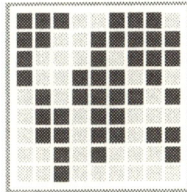

The Corruption Notebooks 2006

Stories From the Worldwide Struggle Against Abuses of Power

Edited by Jonathan Werve
& Global Integrity

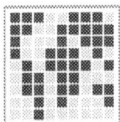

GLOBAL INTEGRITY

Independent Information on Governance & Corruption

THE CORRUPTION NOTEBOOKS 2006.

Phone: +1 (202) 449-4100
Email: info@globalintegrity.org.
Web: www.globalintegrity.org

Global Integrity books may be purchased for educational, business or sales
promotional use. For information please contact Global Integrity.

FIRST EDITION

ISBN 978-0-6151-5212-7

"They will form the most corrupt government on earth,
if the means of their corruption be not prevented."

Thomas Jefferson,
Letter to U. S. President George Washington, 1792

Authors

Shahin Abbasov	Kazadi Mpoyi-Mutombo
Sarah Akrofi-Quarcoo	Njabulo Ncube
Maha Al-Azar	Mutegi Njau
Walid Al-Saqqaf	Akin Olaniyan
Hari Bahadur Thapa	Paul Radu
Salim R. Biryetega	Zoran Radulovic
Michée Boko	Leonarda Reyes
Miomir Brkic	Sebastian Sanga
Naira Bulghadaryan	Daniel Santoro
Sheila Coronel	Ritu Sarin
Camilo de Castro	Yulia Savchenko
Sameh Fawzy Henien	Issa Sharabati
Tamrat Giorgis	Galina Stolyarova
Andreas Harsono	Hamadou Tidiane Sy
Charlie Hughes	Alfred Taban Logune
Mahmood Iqbal	Carlos Tautz
Cheechiay Jablasone	Hari Thapa
Yossi Melman	Stanimir Vaglenov
Jim Morris	Daria Vaisman
Marcelo Mosse	Nargis Zokirova

Editors

Jennifer Frazier, Managing Editor
Elizabeth Brown
Sinziana Demian
Christopher Drosner
Julie Mañes Bostian
Laura Peterson
Carly Schulaka
Jason Van Steenwyk
Beth Walker

Researchers

Ana Bostan
Neil Gordon
Wijayanto

Global Integrity

Nathaniel Heller, Managing Director
Marianne Camerer, International Director
Jonathan Werve, Director of Operations

The Corruption Notebooks is a companion volume to the Global Integrity Report, an annual assessment of governance and corruption worldwide. The Global Integrity Report is available free online (www.globalintegrity.org).

Global Integrity gratefully acknowledges financial support for this project from Legatum Global Development, the Sunrise Foundation, the Wallace Global Fund and the World Bank.

Contents

Introduction   *p. 1*

Argentina   *p. 6*

Armenia   *p. 14*

Azerbaijan   *p. 21*

Benin   *p. 28*

Brazil   *p. 35*

Bulgaria   *p. 41*

Cambodia   *p. 51*

Democratic Republic of Congo   *p. 57*

Arab Republic of Egypt   *p. 62*

Ethiopia   *p. 69*

Georgia   *p. 77*

Ghana   *p. 84*

India   *p. 91*

Indonesia   *p. 98*

Israel   *p. 104*

Kenya   *p. 111*

Kyrgyz Republic   *p. 117*

Lebanon   *p. 124*

Liberia   *p. 132*

Mexico   *p. 139*

Republic of Montenegro *p. 146*

Mozambique *p. 152*

Nepal *P. 158*

Nicaragua *p. 164*

Nigeria *p. 174*

Pakistan *p. 180*

Philippines *p. 187*

Romania *p. 194*

Russian Federation *p. 201*

Senegal *p. 209*

Serbia *p. 215*

Sierra Leone *p. 221*

Sudan *p. 229*

Tajikistan *p. 236*

Tanzania *p. 243*

Uganda *p. 249*

United States *p. 256*

Vietnam *p. 263*

West Bank *p. 271*

Republic of Yemen *p. 276*

Zimbabwe *p. 283*

The Corruption Notebooks 2006

Stories From the Worldwide Struggle Against Abuses of Power

Introduction

These sorts of lofty, introductory chapters typically begin with a quotation from some long-dead thinker invoking democracy, human rights, the rule of law or freedom of the press. This opening ritual serves as a rhetorical echo chamber for the virtues of those institutions and their importance to citizens around the world.

While we certainly don't disagree with those sentiments, this is no longer a time for rhetoric and quotations. It is instead a time of crisis, one that calls for action and courage.

Since the international community began systematically tracking corruption and governance trends in the 1990s, we have witnessed little discernable improvement in the climate of corruption globally, either statistically or anecdotally. In fact, the problem may be getting worse. While developing countries continue to struggle to rein in graft and misuse of public funds, the cancer of corruption increasingly pervades more developed countries as well.

Consider what we have seen in just the past 18 months. A former Western European head of government took a high-paying job with a multinational energy company whose policies he helped advance while in office. Billions of U.S. taxpayer dollars have gone missing in Iraq, with much of the money under no-bid contracts to politically-connected firms. The President of the World Bank (which, in the interest of full disclosure, partially funds Global Integrity) was embroiled in a textbook case of alleged nepotism, after approving a massive pay raise for his girlfriend.

The ostensible leaders of the "free world" frequently implore developing nations to curb corruption, yet fail to keep their own houses in order. How can this leadership inspire the rest of the world to make the tough choices for reform? Such is our time of crisis.

Global Integrity was created in 1999 to provide the public with a set of unbiased, comprehensive toolkits for tracking governance and corruption trends around the world. By combining qualitative, hard hitting journalism with a rigorous, quantitative methodology for capturing the strengths and weaknesses of national anti-corruption systems, we aim to provide policymakers, the business community, journalists, and citizens alike with the information and data they need to effectively advocate for change.

This volume contains the journalistic reporting and analysis that forms part of the 2006 Global Integrity Report, an in-depth analysis of anti-corruption mechanisms in countries around the world. Collaborating with a team of more than 200 experts in 43 countries, we gathered more than 11,000 data points and several hundred thousand words of text in an easy-to-understand guide to the strengths and weaknesses of the analyzed countries' governance systems.

While our dataset, the Integrity Indicators, is used widely by policymakers and donors to analyze and prioritize anti-corruption reform programs, the essays here offer readers the "real life" picture of how corruption looks, tastes, feels and smells in a country. They deliberately step away from the all-too-often sterile and academic analysis of corruption and remind us of corruption's damaging impact on the poor, the disadvantaged and the suffering.

In Tanzania, you'll read how cutting edge HIV test kits were abandoned by the Ministry of Health because a politically-connected businessman secured a contract to import outdated, less precise kits—this in a country wracked by the scourge of HIV/AIDS. Launching a legal investigation into the HIV test kit scandal would likely prove futile; a 2005 public survey indicated that 97 percent of respondents felt corruption in the Tanzanian judiciary was rampant.

In the Philippines, organized crime syndicates engage in widespread bribery of politicians and the police to ensure that their illegal numbers game, the *jueteng*, take in what little earnings the Filipino poor manage to come by. Estimates indicate that 20 to 30 percent of all *jueteng* revenue, which itself is around US$600 million, is spent on bribes or protection money to local mayors, police and other officials—those that should be defending the poor, not benefiting from their exploitation.

And in Vietnam, one of the world's hottest emerging

markets for foreign investors, corruption has become so pervasive that that more than 70 percent of people in the capital Hanoi and more than 65 percent of people in Ho Chi Minh City, the country's two largest cities, are willing to bribe to get things done, according to surveys. At the same time, a staggering one-third of the government workforce admits receiving bribes. All of this occurs in a country where government control and censorship over the media is so complete that our reporter in Vietnam was forced to publish this essay anonymously because of safety concerns.

It is in this somewhat depressing context, a world of growing doubt about our political leaders and their commitment to the public good, that the journalists writing here continue to defend the public interest by speaking truth to power. They refuse to cower under the glare of government scrutiny and harassment. They are proudly part of a shrinking, but more important than ever, group of truth tellers: independent and investigative journalists working in a world increasingly inundated with spin, ideology, and "corporatized" media.

They may be our last defense against corruption.

But they also report reasons for hope. In Mexico, despite deeply-entrenched corruption in the judiciary and the police, average citizens are subject to fewer shakedowns for securing basic services and government paperwork than in the past. In Liberia, a poor country just emerging from a brutal armed conflict, strong political leadership has spurred a change in attitude, contributing to a new environment where, as our reporter writes, "Engaging in corruption under the present administration could be quite a risky venture."

We hope that this body of work inspires readers to action and not just rhetoric: to stand up and speak out against injustice, to support those who are already doing so and to inspire others to believe fervently that accountable and responsive government is the *right* of every citizen, not just the privilege of a few.

Nathaniel Heller

Co-founder &
Managing Director,
Global Integrity

Marianne Camerer

Co-founder &
International Director,
Global Integrity

April 2007

Argentina:
The Silent System
By Daniel Santoro

Every time Argentines fill their cars with gasoline, they
are paying for corruption. Every petrodollar spent in Argentina sends cents to a special account that President Néstor
Kirchner's government manages with little accountability.
Every time Argentines vote, they don't know for sure who
financed their candidate's electoral campaign. Every time
honest Argentines pay taxes, they are paying at rates above
the world average, because they must pay for the thousands
of Argentines who dodge their taxes. The *Impuesto al Valor
Agregado*, the tax on consumption, is a massive 21 percent.

But corruption in Argentina isn't a daily affront on the
lives of its citizens. Argentina is not Russia, where drivers
must routinely pay bribes to the police. In Argentina, the
costs of corruption are hidden, indirect. Many Argentines are
never aware of these silent mechanisms of corruption.

In 2003 the Kirchner government launched a series
of reforms. Kirchner replaced most Supreme Court justices

through a transparent process. The same year saw public access to information law, Ordinance 1172/03.

But the Kirchner administration seems to have forgotten its promises to fight the corruption that ran rampant under President Carlos Menem's rule from 1989 to 1999. Despite positive steps taken early in Kirchner's administration, the government has failed to follow through. Argentina still lacks efficient mechanisms to control and combat corruption.

The government is not alone in this neglect. In 2006, the media is complicit. The press shun a watchdog role and Argentine participation in civil society is low. Interest in public debate is limited. And why bother? Last year, Internal Gross Product increased 9.2 percent—a signal of real economic growth. Our economic well-being, after the deep financial crisis of 2001, increases public tolerance of corruption.

Kirchner's reluctance to confront corruption is directly proportional to the expansion of political hegemony by his government. In the last year, Kirchner's party, *Frente Para la Victoria* (the Front for Victory), won the parliamentary elections. It controls most of the counties and the two *cámeras* (houses) of the congress. Meanwhile, the opposition is divided and increasingly fails to be a credible alternative to government power.

Carlos Manfroni, a former adviser of the Organization of American States on corruption issues, put it this way:

> The Kirchner government's concentration
> of power has two focal points encouraging

ARGENTINA

The Global Integrity Index:
How effective are Argentina's anti-corruption safeguards?

OVERALL RATING
Moderate (79)

CATEGORY RATINGS

1) Civil Society, Public Information & Media — Moderate (73)

2) Elections — Strong (87)

3) Government Accountability — Moderate (71)

4) Administration & Civil Service — Moderate (74)

5) Oversight & Regulation — Strong (85)

6) Anti-Corruption & Rule of Law — Strong (83)

(Scores range from 0 to 100)

The Global Integrity Index, through the Integrity Indicators, assesses the existence and effectiveness of national anti-corruption mechanisms. It does not measure corruption itself (which is nearly impossible). Instead, the Index analyzes the opposite of corruption: the institutions and practices that promote more accountable government and prevent, deter or punish corruption.

The Index is based on nearly 300 Integrity Indicators, discrete scores assigned by local experts using a consistent methodology and scoring criteria for each country. These results are then blindly peer reviewed at the local and international level to ensure consistency and accuracy.

All of the more than 11,000 Integrity Indicator scores that comprise the 2006 Index are published—along with extensive commentary, references and critical peer review comments and perspectives—in the annual Global Integrity Report.

For full results and downloadable datasets, see the Global Integrity website (www.globalintegrity.org).

corruption. First, the concentration of power obstructs the control of corruption. Second, it demands a steady distribution of benefits to the political class, in order to satisfy those who would otherwise protest that concentration. This is especially serious in how it damages Argentina's federal regime through patronage (via distribution of the national budget) to the county governors and the mayors so that they line up behind the Kirchner government.

In concert with Manfroni's warning, in 2006 two civil society organizations petitioned the government. The watchdog groups, Citizen Power (*Poder Ciudadano*) and the Center for the Implementation of Public Policies Promoting Equity and Growth (CIPPEC—*Centro de Implementación de Políticas Públicas para la Equidad y el Crecimiento*) prepared a report on the implementation of the Interamerican Convention Against Corruption of 1996. Their report objects to how the government designated auditors of the state without public competition, government claims to improve the systems to grant public contracts to private companies and a witness protection program for corruption cases, among other measures.

In Argentina there are two administrative organizations that work outside the orbit of the Justice Ministry. The Accounting Office of the State (SIGEN—*Sindicatura General de la Nación*) that reports to the presidency and the General Accounting Office of the Nation (AGN—*Auditoría General de la Nación*) that reports to the Congress.

ARGENTINA

The SIGEN leadership is not promising. The president of SIGEN is Marcelo Moroni, a lawyer and close friend of the head of the cabinet, Alberto Fernández. The vice-president of SIGEN is Alessandra Minnicelli, wife of the Minister of Federal Planning, Julio De Vido.

On the other hand, the president of the AGN is Leandro Despouy, a lawyer of the opposition party (UCR—*Unión Cívica Radical*). However, Despouy has to submit his audits to the vote of a directory where Kirchner's Peronist party holds a majority.

During the UCR party's rule from 1999 to 2001, President Fernando De La Rúa created the Office of the Fight Against the Corruption. The current head of that office, Abel Fleitas Ortiz De Rosas, showed great enthusiasm for investigating cases of corruption during the Menem administration. However, the office has shown little interest in accusations against the Kirchner administration.

To make matters worse, the congressional auditor (directed by Peronist Oscar Lamberto) is years behind schedule in reviewing the government's expenses.

So, yes—laws, organizations and intentions exist to investigate corruption in Argentina, just as the Interamerican Convention against the Corruption demands. But, as Carlos Manfroni suggested, they are slow and toothless.

For example, in June of 2006, the AGN issued a report questioning the lack of controls on delivering 1.6 million pesos (US$517,400) of subsidies to private companies that provide public transportation, like bus companies. The government pays those subsidies to control tickets prices for the millions of poor Argentines who travel in buses every day.

Those 1.6 million pesos don't come from the national budget. They come from a special account called a *fideicommissum* (fiduciary fund). This fund is financed with a special tax on gas. Every Argentine that fuels his or her car is financing that account.

The *fideicommissum* are exempt from the law of Financial Administration, which regulates the expenses of the national budget and establishes various accounting controls. At the moment, there are twenty *fideicommissum* that administer 6 billion pesos per year (US$1.9 billion). That is equal to nearly four percent of the national budget.

AGN's report claimed that the Secretary of Transportation, Ricardo Jaime, played a role in the distribution of this fund. The AGN wanted to know how the private companies spend those 1.6 million pesos. How much do they spend in salaries? How much for fuel?

In addition, the report requested that the government turn over expense reports on an advance of 17 million pesos (US$5.5 million) that Jaime gave to the union of truck drivers which supports Hugo Moyano, president Kirchner's ally.

In his answer to the report, Jaime affirmed that the controls to the subsidies began with his administration in July of 2003, that "the absence of controls was the previous government's responsibility," and that the advance of 17 million pesos to the truck drivers' union was legal.

Two months later, the congressional Commission Parliamentary Reviewer of Accounts still had not revised the AGN report, as required by law. In July 2006, the federal judge,

ARGENTINA

Sergio Torres, finally began requesting information to determine if crimes are committed with these handouts to trucking companies.

This two-month delay was relatively brief, compared to the three years of stalled investigation into illegal campaign financing during the 2003 campaign that elected Kirchner president. As of this writing, the electoral judge María Servini still has not sanctioned the Solidarity Argentina foundation for an illegal $6 million peso (US$1.9 million) donation to former president Carlos Menem's campaign, despite the fact that this event was established in a judicial case.

But secret transfers of money to political parties are far from the only crimes going unpunished in Argentina. In 2005, Santiago Montoya, a Buenos Aires civil servant, uncovered a massive tax scam. He unearthed a novel computer system through which about 250,000 Argentines, politicians among them, used credit cards held at banks registered in other countries. Purchases on these cards are not registered in Argentina. Instead, they went directly to the out-of-country banks, as if the Argentine purchasers were tourists.

This allowed Argentine millionaires to hide their spending from the state and evade taxes. Of the approximately 250,000 Argentines using this system, only 8,000 officially declared the use of out-of-country bank accounts.

Surely the government would investigate this revenue draining scheme? But the Unit of Financial Information (UIF—*Unidad de Información Financiera*), the agency tasked with investigating money laundering, was beheaded at the beginning of 2006. During a round of government infighting, the UIF director was removed, and a new director has yet to be named. In the four years since its creation, the UIF hasn't achieved a single judicial condemnation of money laundering despite 64 accusations presented to the Ministry of Justice.

In Argentina, it is as if the black money flowing through corruption and tax evasion simply does not exist.

For an alternative perspective, read the critical peer review commentary on this notebook, part of the 2006 Global Integrity Report (www.globalintegrity.org).

ARGENTINA

Armenia:
The Bureaucrats' Web
By Naira Bulghadaryan

"I am not guilty. My employees were careless and unreli-
able," said a head of an Armenian social service department
about the illegitimate actions going on under his supervision. In fact, it was under his very nose that a 154,088 dram
(US$400) poverty allowance had been issued to a family that
did not meet the government's standards to receive it. The
three employees who undertook the forgery received only
a warning, as did the social inspector, who had previously
forged similar papers for other citizens.

Karine, a 50-year-old resident of Vanadzor, Armenia's
third-largest city, agreed to give three months of her poverty
allowance to the employees of social services so that her family could at least get something. Last year she gave 23,113
dram (US$60). This year the inspectors demanded 38,522
dram (US$100), a very big sum for someone who has no
other income. I asked her why she paid the bribe if she was
entitled to the full allowance. "What can I do?" she said,

"they would find every reason to deprive me of it."

The lack of knowledge is the primary cause of these common occurrences. "If you are not aware of the laws and of your rights, they will easily take advantage of you," Karine said, indicating an implicit tolerance of the inspectors' methods. "They will tell you that you do not have the status of beneficiary, and that if you complain to their superiors they will deprive you of what you have."

The beneficiaries of allowances complain that every four months they must leave the payments—anywhere from 6,500 dram to 28,000 dram (US$17 to US$73) a year—in the post office, the same place where they receive payments. They have to sign a "don't pay" note under their name and come home without their usual allowance. If they protest, they are caught in a bureaucratic cobweb of trouble. They might, for example, be sent endlessly from one office to another, or their condominium might refuse to give them a certificate of residence. Citizens thus agree to leave some money behind.

"My poor and sick neighbor has to leave some of his allowance in the post office all the time, and he complains about this illegal process," said 25-year-old economist Arthur Karapetyan. In order to defend his neighbor's rights, Karapetyan addressed an appeal to the Ministry of Labor and Social Affairs in August 2005. Thirteen people joined the protest, among them beneficiaries, pensioners and disabled citizens. Each of them left 770 dram (US$2) from their monthly pensions. Karapetyan informed the officials who were following the traces of complaints that the money "extracted" from the allowances amounted to 19 million dram (US$50,000) a month. The officials of the ministry could not

The Global Integrity Index:
How effective are Armenia's anti-corruption safeguards?

OVERALL RATING
Very Weak (54)

CATEGORY RATINGS
1) Civil Society, Public Information & Media — Weak (63)

2) Elections — Weak (62)

3) Government Accountability — Very Weak (46)

4) Administration & Civil Service — Very Weak (29)

5) Oversight & Regulation — Weak (69)

6) Anti-Corruption & Rule of Law — Very Weak (57)

(Scores range from 0 to 100)

The Global Integrity Index, through the Integrity Indicators, assesses the existence and effectiveness of national anti-corruption mechanisms. It does not measure corruption itself (which is nearly impossible). Instead, the Index analyzes the opposite of corruption: the institutions and practices that promote more accountable government and prevent, deter or punish corruption.

The Index is based on nearly 300 Integrity Indicators, discrete scores assigned by local experts using a consistent methodology and scoring criteria for each country. These results are then blindly peer reviewed at the local and international level to ensure consistency and accuracy.

All of the more than 11,000 Integrity Indicator scores that comprise the 2006 Index are published—along with extensive commentary, references and critical peer review comments and perspectives—in the annual Global Integrity Report.

For full results and downloadable datasets, see the Global Integrity website (www.globalintegrity.org).

refute these data, which came from reliable sources within the social system. As a result, 17 employees of the Social Insurance Fund were reprimanded, and seven were dismissed.

Corruption is widespread not only in the social welfare system, but also in health care. State policy supports socially dependent and sick people such as 55-year-old Sirush. Sirush had 14 operations and half of her intestines removed, but when she requested a degree of disability, she was told to wait. "Maybe my intestines will grow again?" she asked the nurse in surprise.

Armine wanted to request a degree of disability for her 6-year-old son, who was blind of one eye. With his medical certificate in hand, she approached the commission of experts, but she was not granted her request. "They told me that my child's state was not that bad after all," Armine said, "and they concluded that my son could only receive a degree of disability if he stopped seeing with his second eye as well."

The bribe for a degree of disability varies, depending on the level of the illness, the place of residence and the appetite of the commission. According to Arthur Petrosyan, the appetite of Artashes Ananyan, head of the second medical-social commission of the capital city Yerevan, was limited to 154,089 dram (US$400). He allegedly asked for that amount to restore Petrosyan to the third level of disability. Ananyan's partner, Karine Asrya, head of the Radiotherapy Center of the Ministry of Health, was allegedly satisfied with 77,044 dram (US$200) to give Petrosyan the necessary documents. In June 2006, Petrosyan pressed charges against the two doctors. The case is now in court.

Delivery of medical aid for pregnant women is sup-

ARMENIA

posed to be free of charge in Armenia. "We are just used to showing our gratitude to doctors for their kindness, following the voluntary-obligatory principle," says Lilit, who had a baby last year. "Otherwise the mother and her newborn baby will be subjected to indifference, and then they will have to spend even more money to be restored to health." The expression "Congratulations!" has its cost. Depending on what town you live in, it costs from 11,556 dram to 19,261 dram (US$30 to US$50) to deliver a baby. Vanadzor resident Levon gave 19,261 dram (US$50) to the serving staff, 38,552 dram (US$100) to the doctor and paid 1,155 dram to 1,926 dram (US$3 to US$5) a day for the care of the mother and her child. In short, having a baby costs an Armenian 77,044 dram to 192,661 dram (US$200 to US$500).

Expenses grow along with the child. Armine's two daughters attend one of the central schools of Vanadzor. From their small family budget of 19,261 dram (US$50), the family has to spend 3,852 dram to 7,704 dram (US$10 to US$20) each month on presents for teachers and on maintenance costs in the classrooms. They must even pay the cleaning lady so she cleans the floor for their children.

"Every year the state allocates to schools 8.5 million dram (US$22,000) for maintenance and repairs costs" says Mayis Khachatryan, Lori region representative of the Ministry of Education and Science. But the schools also take money from students. I asked her if the schools had the right to use the money in any way they wanted. "A liar is a liar everywhere, I don't know," says Khachatryan.

After the school years, the struggle with the Higher Education Institution begins. The bribe for entrance examinations starts at 577,834 dram (US$1,500) and grows depending on the quality of the institution you will attend and on the demand for the profession desired. Last year Sh. M., lecturer of Vanadzor State Teachers' Training Institute, was charged with taking bribes and was imprisoned, only to be set free a few days later.

Economist Eduard Aghajanov estimates that 385 billion dram (US$1 billion) of "black money" circulates yearly in Armenia.

According to a survey by Transparency International Armenia, the major reasons for corruption in Armenian society are the unfavorable social-economic conditions, anarchy and impunity of authorities. Amalya Kostanyan, head of the nongovernmental organization's Armenia chapter, says the country is marred by "political retributions," and that those who rise against the authorities will be punished for corruption. She mentions the case of Vahe Grigoryan, a lawyer who has been in prison since February 2006, on forgery charges. Ms. Kostanyan claims that Mr. Grigoryan was imprisoned for daring to struggle against illegal construction in the center of Yerevan in which the government forced people to sell their houses.

People who own small and medium-sized businesses know that without the support of well-placed officials, they face an uphill struggle for business. Martun Alikhanyan, whose business manufactures machine tools, does not dream about expansion. "They won't allow me," he says, mentioning a member of parliament who tried to establish a business importing sugar. "They made the tax and duty field work against him, and also against the ones who would sell his

ARMENIA

goods," says Alikhanyan. He gave the names of several MPs, such as Gagik Tsarukyan, Samvel Alexanyan, Lyova Sargsyan, Khachatur Sukiasyan, who control the import of flour, sugar, fuel and other goods into Armenia. Although the Constitution states that an MP is not entitled to own a business, this provision hasn't prevented MP Vahram Baghdasaryan from establishing a TV station, founding a business complex and selling syrup to the army.

"If you work in a legal way, you'll work with a loss," said M. Ch., one of the former heads of tax department of Vanadzor. According to him, for the circulation of goods worth 77,044 dram (US$200) taxes will be half that amount. "Add to that US$100 for sanitary epidemic station, US$50 for fire department, US$1 or US$2 for policemen, US$50 bribe to inspectors of municipality and tax department, and your loss will exceed US$150," said Mr. Ch. He believes that an imperfect legislative field and a system based on nepotism are the reasons for 70 percent of Armenia's shadow economy.

The anti-corruption laws that have been adopted in Armenia have remained only on paper, or used solely against the opposition. During the three years since an anti-corruption effort was launched, no high-ranking officials have been punished. Corruption has deep roots in Armenian society, and political resolve will not arise without pressure from the public.

For an alternative perspective, read the critical peer review commentary on this notebook, part of the 2006 Global Integrity Report (www.globalintegrity.org).

Azerbaijan:
The Price of Gratitude

By Shain Abbasov

Two months ago, my friend Ulviya told me a frightening story about the events that transpired after her 26-year-old brother was fatally hit by a car in Azerbaijan. "The relatives of the driver first offered compensation to withdraw our claim," she said. "We refused, but the court finally decided that my brother committed suicide by throwing himself in front of the car, and the guy who killed him avoided punishment. As we found out later, [the driver's relatives] paid the investigator and judge [17,601 manat] US$20,000."

When Azerbaijan obtained independence in the fall of 1991, we young students were full of hope for the future prosperity of our country. No one imagined the difficulties the country would face in its first 15 years of independence.

Today, people face bribery from the day they are born until the day they die. Although a free public health system officially exists, delivering a child in a maternity hospital costs parents between 264 manat and 440 manat (US$300 and US$500), depending on the clinic and the doctor's reputation. The documents marking the first and last moments of one's life cannot be obtained without money. In addition to the official duty for birth certificates, relatives have to pay so-called *hermet* (respect) fees of nine manat (US$10) or more to national registry office employees. Worse, bribes must be paid to cemetery administrators for a burial site: At some central cemeteries in the capital city of Baku, these can run up to 2640 manat (US$3,000).

The 2005 Transparency International Corruption Perception Index ranked Azerbaijan 137th out of 146 countries. Experts have estimated the cost of corruption in Azerbaijan at several billion dollars per year, a level approaching the country's total budget of 3.5 billion manat (US$4 billion) in 2006. This entrenched malfeasance keeps the country's citizens mired in poverty: The average monthly income in Azerbaijan is only 131 manat (US$148.50), ranging from 174 manat (US$198) in Baku to 87 manat (US$99) in the rest of the country, and some 29 percent of Azerbaijanis live on less than 2 manat (US$2) per day. One of the main reasons for Azerbaijan's endemic corruption is its flawed separation of powers. Executive power dominates in this authoritarian country, and the inability of parliamentarians and judicial authorities to resist corruption create links in a vicious cycle.

Everything in the judicial courts is for sale. Shortening prison sentences costs about 1,760 manat (US$2,000) per year. In 2005 Supreme Court judge was caught releasing a prisoner early. The judge kept his job, although three justice ministry officials were convicted in the case. Any lawyer will tell you that any court judgment can be fought at a cost of tens of thousands of dollars, depending on the weight of the criminal offence or value of disputed property. For example, suspending a traffic accident investigation costs 880 manat (US$1,000); dismissing a criminal case, 2,200 manat to 3,520 manat (US$2,500 to US$4,000); overriding substantial evidence in a judgment, 44,003 manat (US$50,000).

Azerbaijanis learn about corruption early: Where people around the world pay to be taught, in Azerbaijan they pay to remain uneducated. If a high school student gets a grade of three—equivalent to an American 'C'—on his 8th grade final, his parents can pay about 176 manat (US$200) to upgrade. Prices increase at universities. Depending on the popularity of the university or department, passing an exam or getting a good score costs students between 22 manat and 264 manat (US$25 and US$300). Professors who don't want to waste time have been known to present students with their "price list." Even well-prepared students often pay to get into the next grade.

In 2005, a student group called the *Dalga* (Wave) Youth Organization conducted a survey of 5,000 students. The survey that identified bribing as students' biggest problem. The organization also listed the most corrupt universities in Azerbaijan. "It turned out that only four universities out of about 70 don't accept bribes," said *Dalga* leader Ramin Hajili. The survey results inspired *Dalga* to launch a public campaign called "Education without Bribes."

"We openly blackmailed professors and chancellors through public statements: 'If you continue to demand bribes

The Global Integrity Index:
How effective are Azerbaijan's anti-corruption safeguards?

OVERALL RATING

Very Weak (60)

CATEGORY RATINGS

1) Civil Society, Public Information & Media — Weak (69)

2) Elections — Weak (65)

3) Government Accountability — Very Weak (44)

4) Administration & Civil Service — Very Weak (44)

5) Oversight & Regulation — Moderate (73)

6) Anti-Corruption & Rule of Law — Weak (65)

(Scores range from 0 to 100)

The Global Integrity Index, through the Integrity Indicators, assesses the existence and effectiveness of national anti-corruption mechanisms. It does not measure corruption itself (which is nearly impossible). Instead, the Index analyzes the opposite of corruption: the institutions and practices that promote more accountable government and prevent, deter or punish corruption.

The Index is based on nearly 300 Integrity Indicators, discrete scores assigned by local experts using a consistent methodology and scoring criteria for each country. These results are then blindly peer reviewed at the local and international level to ensure consistency and accuracy.

All of the more than 11,000 Integrity Indicator scores that comprise the 2006 Index are published—along with extensive commentary, references and critical peer review comments and perspectives—in the annual Global Integrity Report.

For full results and downloadable datasets, see the Global Integrity website (www.globalintegrity.org).

we publish the list,'" Hajili said. However, the campaign resulted in some unexpected negative outcomes. "In some universities where professors were threatened, they increased bribe rates because of the increased risk, and now some students call us 'troublemakers,'" Hajili said.

The Azerbaijani parliament introduced a new anti-corruption law in 2004 and increased penalties for corruption in 2006. Though the Commission on Fighting Corruption was established in 2005, not a single important case has been launched, and most of the cases it has opened appear politically motivated. In one case, a former economic development minister, who was fired and arrested in 2005 for cooperating with opposition forces that were planning a coup, was later accused by the commission of illegally privatizing national companies in the 1990s.

While the oil and gas industry is the most profitable in Azerbaijan, it is also among the least transparent. In 2005, the Baku-based magazine Hesabat published figures on office-supply procurement by the State Oil Company of Azerbaijan (SOCAR), which provides more than 60 percent of the state's revenue. Prices paid under the contract were 10 times higher than market rates: Lamps that cost 0.22 qepik (US$0.25) at any Baku shop were purchased for about 4 manat (US$5). Tellingly, the publication did not prompt an investigation and no one was punished.

Some improvements are visible. Azerbaijan's new president, Ilham Aliyev, understands poverty's potential threat to the stability of the ruling elite, so his government has taken steps to improve the country's socio-economic situation. A huge inflow of oil revenues from high oil prices allowed the government to significantly increase state employee wages, decreasing day-to-day corruption. For example, the number of roadside bribes has decreased significantly since traffic police wages tripled in 2005. "Now traffic policemen stop you for real violations, and in most cases they refuse to take bribes and impose a legal fine," said Alekper Aliyev, a taxi driver in Baku.

Getting a new passport or changing an old one used to mean waiting in long lines in front of the police department and paying a 13 manat bribe (US$15) for quick document processing. When I changed my passport in April 2006, the line was well organized, policemen were helpful and not even small bribes were demanded. However, obtaining my ID card the same month in the local police branch cost about 26 manat (US$30).

Customs, tax services and the pension system have also reportedly improved. Anarchy no longer reigns at Baku International airport, where customs and border control officers once charged ordinary citizens between nine manat and 132 manat (US$10 and US$150) to enter and exit the country.

Though some things have changed for the better, ordinary Azerbaijanis are themselves to blame for the systemic corruption that has become part of their culture. According to one survey, 59.9 percent of people in Azerbaijan admitted to being happy to pay bribes in order to solve their problems quickly. About 90 percent of the Azerbaijani population pay or receive bribes, the survey found.

"I am against paying bribes," said a friend, Farid

Arifoglu, who recently had a baby. "But when I was getting a birth certificate for my son, I had to 'thank' an employee of the registrar with [nine manat] US$10. The mood there is paradoxical. Those who don't pay hermet feel guilty. It's hard to explain, but it's probably an issue of mentality. When it's a happy occasion you have to share your joy, in this case financially."

For an alternative perspective, read the critical peer review commentary on this notebook, part of the 2006 Global Integrity Report (www.globalintegrity.org).

AZERBAIJAN

Benin:
A New Start

By Michée Boko

Chronicling the culture of corruption in Benin would have been an easy task under the government of former President Mathieu Kérékou. Numerous economic and financial scandals plagued Kérékou's more than three decades of rule, which came to an end in April 2006. However, since President Yayi Boni's landslide election, the new leader has made significant headway in reducing the impunity that marked his predecessor's administration.

The battle cry of Boni's campaign was, *"Ça peut changer! Ça doit changer! Ça va changer!"* meaning, "It can change! It must change! It will change!" Nearly 75 percent of the electorate agreed with the former development banker. Boni is now implementing major changes to the way public affairs are led—beginning by holding past officials accountable for their alleged crimes.

Under Kérékou's long-time rule (1972-1991 and 1996-2006), the people of Benin had become accustomed to public officials using their positions for private gain and facing little or no consequences. For example, with the approval of Kérékou's Minister of Foreign Affairs, Rogatien Biaou, a piece of land belonging to the Benin Embassy in the United States, was sold without the government's consent. Biaou was arrested for a brief period in early 2006 and then released. As a member of the government, Biaou could not be tried without parliamentary approval.

Now, however, the case is pending in front of the High Court of Justice, which is the only court with the authority to try members of the government. Biaou's accomplices are already in jail and the minister should be tried soon.

Biaou's case is hardly unique. In July 2006, the Parliament sent Alain Adihou, another minister in the Kérékou administration, in front of the High Court of Justice for misuse of public funds. Adihou's ministry had been allocated funds to create a *Liste Electorale Permanente Informatisée* (Computerized Permanent Electoral Roll). Adihou never completed the project and large sums of the money disappeared.

A third minister of the Kérékou government, Cosme Sèhlin, was also arrested in July 2006 after Boni's election. Police reported finding large sums of illegally obtained money—amounting to approximately 20.8 billion francs (US$40 million)—and other undisclosed, illegally procured and prohibited products in his home. The corruption characteristic of the Kérékou administration was not contained just to the public sector. In June 2006, Justice officials arrested Séfou Fagbohoun, a prominent businessman, who was said to be untouchable under Kérékou. Fagbohoun is accused of

The Global Integrity Index:
How effective are Benin's anti-corruption safeguards?

OVERALL RATING
Moderate (79)

CATEGORY RATINGS

1) Civil Society, Public Information & Media — Strong (80)

2) Elections — Strong (80)

3) Government Accountability — Moderate (71)

4) Administration & Civil Service — Weak (68)

5) Oversight & Regulation — Strong (89)

6) Anti-Corruption & Rule of Law — Strong (87)

(Scores range from 0 to 100)

The Global Integrity Index, through the Integrity Indicators, assesses the existence and effectiveness of national anti-corruption mechanisms. It does not measure corruption itself (which is nearly impossible). Instead, the Index analyzes the opposite of corruption: the institutions and practices that promote more accountable government and prevent, deter or punish corruption.

The Index is based on nearly 300 Integrity Indicators, discrete scores assigned by local experts using a consistent methodology and scoring criteria for each country. These results are then blindly peer reviewed at the local and international level to ensure consistency and accuracy.

All of the more than 11,000 Integrity Indicator scores that comprise the 2006 Index are published—along with extensive commentary, references and critical peer review comments and perspectives—in the annual Global Integrity Report.

For full results and downloadable datasets, see the Global Integrity website (www.globalintegrity.org).

mismanaging the national gas company (SONACOP—*Société Nationale de Commercialisation des Produits Pétroliers*), which he purchased under questionable circumstances. He is also accused of tax evasion, tax fraud and other white-collar crimes. Several high-ranking police officers have also been incarcerated for embezzlement since Boni took office.

"During the time of Mathieu Kérékou, you could see spreading corruption. You could see its effects on the economy, on new investment initiatives, on the life of citizens, it was obvious," said Pascal Todjinou, secretary general of the General Confederation of Benin Workers (CGTB—*Confédération Générale Des Travailleurs du Bénin*).

Since his inauguration on April 6, 2006, Boni has shown the Beninese people that he plans to follow through on his promises for widespread reform, not only holding past officials accountable, but also by stressing the importance of integrity within his own administration.

"The president clearly told his ministers—who repeated this to us—that if they ever got involved in any kind of corruption, they better resign before he gets to know what happened," said Jean-Baptiste Elias, a prominent corruption fighter and president of the *Observatoire de Lutte contre la Corruption* (Observatory to Fight Corruption), a publicly funded government watchdog group.

In his electoral campaign program, Boni wrote: "Eradication of economical delinquency is a short-term objective. We will take immediate good governance measures in order to eradicate corruption in all sectors…What will also change is the method of governance. While focusing on values such

BENIN

as rigor, civism, discipline, respect to public goods, ethics, obligation to accountable to the nation and obligation to bear results, our method of work will leave no place to impunity."

In April, shortly after taking office, Boni and the members of his administration publicly disclosed their personal assets. Although the disclosure of high-ranking government officials' private interests is stipulated in the Constitution, this was the first time the information was made public by so many government officials. Observers saw the move by the president as an early sign of transparency. The Boni administration also has adopted a code of ethics, which bans the practice of corruption from the government.

In June, Boni reactivated the State Inspector General, which he charged with investigating corruption wherever it happens, regardless of who is involved. The State Inspector General replaced the ineffective *Cellule de Moralisation de la Vie Publique* (Public Life Moralisation Unit) which worked, without results, for 10 years (1996-2006) under the Kérékou administration. During those 10 years, corruption simply grew and grew.

"It became a national sport," said trade union activist Francis Hounsou.

Although Benin's Council of Ministers has gone as far as to institute a national day against corruption to combat graft, corruption continues to be entrenched in many aspects of Beninese daily life.

"We noticed that the tax departments, the customs, the police, the gendarmes and the harbour of Cotonou are the places where corruption is very high in Benin," Elias said.

"Public contracts, justice and recently, the new decentralized administrations are also corruption poles."

Police still demand money on the road from taxi drivers, even if drivers have the correct documents. Custom officers keep on taking bribes from clients, and politicians continue to buy positive stories from willing journalists.

"Some people are born and raised in corruption. They can't pay their rent, pay their bills and run their car without corruption. So, don't expect those people to immediately give up corruption," Todjinou said.

Custom officers are known to be particularly corrupt and resistant.

"It does not matter how honest you are or how correct is your business. The custom officers will [force] you to [pay bribes to] them, or you will not get through the customs and have your goods out," complained a businessman at an official meeting with the head of state at the Presidential Palace on July 29, 2006.

Secretary General of the Chamber of Trade and Industry, Chakirou Tidjani, explained that custom officers often take advantage of merchants' rush to get their often perishable products on the market by slowing the process and thereby forcing the businesses to pay bribes or risk loosing profits.

Due to Boni's reforms, however, it is becoming increasingly difficult for custom officers to demand bribes, Elias said. He added, however, that the officers have found a new way to get the money: by overtaxing the goods in order to force the client to negotiate a fairer price. In the negotiation, the officers receive the money they are chasing.

BENIN

"The men of the old system are still in place. Only members of government have changed," Elias said. "But we got a strong signal from the president that impunity will decrease. Those who used to think that they are untouchable will soon face justice. Corruption, bad governance and embezzlements will no longer remain unpunished like in the past."

For an alternative perspective, read the critical peer review commentary on this notebook, part of the 2006 Global Integrity Report (www.globalintegrity.org).

Brazil:
The Cynical Code

By Carlos Tautz

To sever the grip of corruption, Brazilians must break an unwritten law—Gerson's law. It is an amoral and unwritten social regulation that is widely accepted: it's okay to bribe, cheat and take advantage of every situation.

The phrase was made famous across Brazil in a TV cigarette commercial from the 1970s and 1980s, starring Gerson, a *futebol* (soccer) player who was shown smoking a cigarette and saying, "Take advantage of every situation to get ahead."

Now, 21 years after democracy was formally re-inaugurated in Brazil, Gerson's law frequently comes to mind. Each new political and financial scandal is, in effect, a consequence of this cynical axiom: take advantage of every situation to get what you want.

The following cases are perfect examples:

In 1994, a minister bribed federal deputies to vote for a constitutional amendment to permit presidential re-election.

The same government was accused of accepting bribes from the U.S. company Raytheon, said to have close ties to the White House and the Pentagon. In the end, Raytheon won a bid against French firm Alsthom to install a multi-billion dollar radar system across the Amazon.

Some thought these occurrences would disappear as Brazil's new democracy took root.

But 11 years after those scandals, new scandals hit the front pages last year. The only difference is that the country is now ruled by opponents of the previous corrupt administration. The bad news is, instead of changing the government, the new congress has simply taken up where its defeated opponents left off.

One scandal involved selling ambulances at artificially increased prices to the health ministry. In another, 62 deputies and senators (out of 553) were caught trading votes for cash. The good news is that five of them resigned, and only 12 won re-election to congress in October's elections.

Brazilian voters are increasingly aware of and educated about corruption because of press coverage over the last four years. The media increased its coverage of corruption, even to the point that some now think that corruption, not the disparate concentration of income, is the worst of Brazil's problems. (Most Brazilians do still identify the disparity of wealth as the country's biggest problem.)

Luis Navarro is head of the corruption prevention and strategic information unit at the Federal Comptroller-General's Office (CGU—*Controladoria Geral da União*), a federal watchdog agency. "As to the causes of corruption, we must say it is a bit cultural. Still, we just can't wait for a solution to fall down from heaven. We must invest in instruments, like the CGU, to prevent and punish corruption," said Navarro.

The CGU itself is a part of democratic advancement. Created in 2001 and strengthened in 2003, the CGU has become a key state institution, tracking the billions of reais the federal government annually sends to almost 6,000 municipalities.

But the structure of the CGU puts it at risk for corrupt activity. The CGU general controller is nominated by the president, which makes the CGU a state-run instrument that may eventually be affected by political interests.

Fortunately, this has not been the case to date. The ambulance scheme, for example, was discovered through CGU periodic audits. The federal police widened the investigation. Both supplied evidence to a parliamentary investigation commission.

"Corruption is part of a badly formed political system, which also involves illegal funding for electoral campaigns," Navarro said. He believes the participation of watchdog civic organizations is important in exposing these problems.

One of these organizations is the Brazilian Budget Forum (FBO—*Fórum Brasil de Orçamento*), a network of organizations, trade unions and other non-governmental institutions that has been tracking the federal budget and

BRAZIL

The Global Integrity Index:
How effective are Brazil's anti-corruption safeguards?

OVERALL RATING
Moderate (73)

CATEGORY RATINGS

1) Civil Society, Public Information & Media — Weak (68)

2) Elections — Strong (84)

3) Government Accountability — Moderate (72)

4) Administration & Civil Service — Weak (66)

5) Oversight & Regulation — Moderate (74)

6) Anti-Corruption & Rule of Law — Moderate (72)

(Scores range from 0 to 100)

The Global Integrity Index, through the Integrity Indicators, assesses the existence and effectiveness of national anti-corruption mechanisms. It does not measure corruption itself (which is nearly impossible). Instead, the Index analyzes the opposite of corruption: the institutions and practices that promote more accountable government and prevent, deter or punish corruption.

The Index is based on nearly 300 Integrity Indicators, discrete scores assigned by local experts using a consistent methodology and scoring criteria for each country. These results are then blindly peer reviewed at the local and international level to ensure consistency and accuracy.

All of the more than 11,000 Integrity Indicator scores that comprise the 2006 Index are published—along with extensive commentary, references and critical peer review comments and perspectives—in the annual Global Integrity Report.

For full results and downloadable datasets, see the Global Integrity website (www.globalintegrity.org).

spending in Brazil since 1991.

"Transparency of government leads to the best practices in public administration, but is far from enough," said João Sucupira, an economist and one of FBO's founders. He also serves as director of the Brazilian Institute of Social and Economic Analysis (IBASE—*Instituto Brasileiro de Análises Sociais e Econômicas*).

"Corruption is only part of the problem. Another problem relates to corruption's influence on Brazil's democracy," said Sucupira.

"Yes, corruption influences the level of democracy in our country...It dishonors political activity," admitted Navarro.

In 1988, the Public Defense Ministry (PM—*Ministério Público*) became a "fourth power" in the Brazilian legal system. Its mandate is to independently investigate matters involving the public interest. This puts the PM at the explosive conjunction of corruption and threats to Brazil's democracy.

The PM's anti-corruption crusade has partly succeeded: in April of this year the general attorney legally denounced 40 of the federal administration's highest officials, including ministers, for corruption.

"The corruption problem is a direct consequence of the perverse concentration of income in Brazil," says Gilda Carvalho, general vice attorney of the federal PM. She believes that most of the corruption is primarily due to the country's new democracy—in place since 1988. "We have much more transparency, more public information than we had 23 years ago, when I entered the PM," she adds.

As the gross national product increases and Brazil

BRAZIL

integrates into the world economy, Carvalho focuses on the financial system as a potential source of corruption. She believes that, to fight corruption, the country needs greater communication and cooperation across governmental agencies.

Carvalho uncovered Brazil's largest financial scandals, which were investigated by the Congress and the PM. The investigation concluded in December 2004, with an explosive final report finding that 91 people, including federal deputies, a former president and directors of the Central Bank were involved in illegal transfers of more than 150.8 billion reais (US$70 billion) between 1996 and 2002 through the Banestado regional bank.

The Banestado scandal also involved wealthy citizens who used the bank to avoid the Brazilian tax system. These citizens included politicians, businessmen, financiers, actors and football players—bringing to mind, once again, the TV ad of the famous soccer player, Gerson.

Gerson's law, though still powerful, is starting to weaken as Brazil's federal and state corruption watchdog agencies grow stronger.

For an alternative perspective, read the critical peer review commentary on this notebook, part of the 2006 Global Integrity Report (www.globalintegrity.org).

Bulgaria:
The Dog Food Dealmakers

By Stanimir Vaglenov

"I'd better be a vegetarian!" The thought crosses my mind as I start working on the shady serial trade deal, which this time concerns the illegal import of 75 tons of beef, kept at the Bulgarian border on its way from Greece. I'm thinking "vegetarian" because this particular meat, coming from far-away Ireland, is 20 years old! The standard in the European Union and in Bulgaria specifies that meat is fit for human consumption no more than two years after it has been produced.

Although the 75 tons of beef had been kept at the border since February 2006, a previous load of 50 tons, imported by the same company, entered the country in December 2005 and was distributed on the market during the Christmas season.

Angry questions have flooded the newspapers: Who is the importer? Who allowed the import? Where were the regulators? How long will it continue to be like this? But this story is old and already well-known. For a long time, the scenario has been the same: a Bulgarian phantom company manages to import goods with disputable quality, because it is supported by a group of bribable customs officers, border policemen and veterinarian inspectors at a border checkpoint in Kulata. Such incidents are common at all Bulgarian borders, a practice that threatens the lives and health of ordinary people. And despite authorities' attempts to change the situation, keeping in mind the forthcoming accession to the European Union, there are no significant signs of change for the better.

Eighty office workers have been dismissed for breaking bribery laws during the first six months of 2006, according to a report presented by Rumen Petkov, the minister of Internal Affairs. For the same period, 150 office workers were caught receiving bribes, were involved in venality schemes or showed sings of tolerating corrupt practices. Despite the gravity of charges, their sentences are symbolic. According to data from the Bulgarian nongovernmental organization Center for the Study of Democracy, 75 percent of the punishments for corruption are imprisonment for a maximum of three years.

According to a May 2006 government report on national security, 2,476 crimes connected with corrupt practices were revealed in 2005, including 105 government employees caught taking bribes. A sociological survey prepared by the Center for the Study of Democracy reports that at least 130,000 corrupt deals take place in Bulgaria every year.

I ask myself how many tons of meat have been distributed in Bulgaria under the above-mentioned scheme. The case with the "20-year-old food for dogs," which was the description of the beef when it was exported from Ireland to the Netherlands, and which was then presented as fit for human consumption at the Bulgarian-Greek border, is just the tip of the iceberg.

During the ensuing investigation, which lasted for several months, I discovered that the owner of the company Bul Impex, the importer of the beef, is Georgy Georgiev. A 35-year-old businessman, Georgiev appears to be the owner of more than 30 other firms, according to the trade registry Ciela. The same companies have more than 35 million leva (approximately US$22 million) in liabilities to the state budget, according to the list of big debtors published on the website of the Ministry of Finance. Georgiev appears to have been playing the role of a postbox, where "enterprising" businessmen have just "dropped" their firms by selling them through fake deals. He then made hundreds of contraband deals, robbing the state budget of millions of leva. For such a result to be accomplished, corrupt state office workers at the border are not enough. More players in the team are needed, such as representatives of Bulgarian taxation authorities. They are extremely rigorous and strict when dealing with ordinary people, who count their last cents just to pay their obligations to the budget. Some state employees, though, are particularly servile toward the "businessmen" who are willing to pay a generous bribe in order to protect their real liabilities from the state.

On July 3, 2005, a venal tax collector, who was also an inspector from Territory Tax Directorate in Sofia, was dismissed. She had been detained two months earlier, caught

BULGARIA

The Global Integrity Index:
How effective are Bulgaria's anti-corruption safeguards?

OVERALL RATING
Moderate (80)

CATEGORY RATINGS

1) Civil Society, Public Information & Media — Strong (84)

2) Elections — Strong (88)

3) Government Accountability — Moderate (73)

4) Administration & Civil Service — Weak (61)

5) Oversight & Regulation — Very Strong (90)

6) Anti-Corruption & Rule of Law — Strong (83)

(Scores range from 0 to 100)

The Global Integrity Index, through the Integrity Indicators, assesses the existence and effectiveness of national anti-corruption mechanisms. It does not measure corruption itself (which is nearly impossible). Instead, the Index analyzes the opposite of corruption: the institutions and practices that promote more accountable government and prevent, deter or punish corruption.

The Index is based on nearly 300 Integrity Indicators, discrete scores assigned by local experts using a consistent methodology and scoring criteria for each country. These results are then blindly peer reviewed at the local and international level to ensure consistency and accuracy.

All of the more than 11,000 Integrity Indicator scores that comprise the 2006 Index are published—along with extensive commentary, references and critical peer review comments and perspectives—in the annual Global Integrity Report.

For full results and downloadable datasets, see the Global Integrity website (www.globalintegrity.org).

with a 5,000 leva (US$3,300) bribe. An investigation proved something already well known: The woman owned several apartments, country homes and a nice car, which she could never have afforded with her official income.

A day later, Chief Tax Inspector Nikolai Popov announced that authorities were working on four more similar cases with taxation employees suspected to be involved in corrupt practices or being exposed to a corrupt pressure. For the first time since the General Tax Directorate was established, it officially announced a telephone line where people could report corruption among taxation agents.

I was almost inclined to believe that Bulgarian clerks were ready to make a real effort and fight corruption, when a new case shook my faith. On Jan. 16, 2006, a BMW SUV with an official plate, registered under the name of Svetlin Mihailov, chief of Sofia City Court, provoked a scandal in the Supreme Court Council. It was revealed that Mihailov had received the car for free from the Customs Service, but that subsequently Rumen Nenkov, deputy chief of the Supreme Court of Cassation, appealed that this order be revoked. As it turned out, the SUV was registered to a German citizen, from whom it had been stolen. When the vehicle passed the Bulgarian border, it was detained by a vigilant customs officer but never returned to its owner. The car became material evidence and had to be kept until the case was solved (which would take at least three or four years at the routine pace of the court system in Bulgaria). Through another well established practice in Bulgaria, customs authorities place such vehicles at the disposal of high-powered state officials—in this

BULGARIA

case, Mihailov. The magistrate fought fiercely for several days to keep the luxury SUV, but the social opinion in Bulgaria and Germany was so ill-disposed toward him that he finally was forced to give up.

At the beginning of February, a list with names of 30 magistrates suspected of corrupt practices was deposited in the chief prosecutor's office. The existence of the list was announced by the Director of The National Investigation Service, Angel Alexandrov. The list contained mostly names of investigators, but also names of judges from around the country. Imputed were cases of thefts, rapes and beatings, in which investigators had failed to do their jobs, until and unless they were paid by the people who were seeking justice.

In February, shortly after the beef incident at the border checkpoint in Kulata, I concluded that corruption in Bulgaria had no boundaries. In Sofia, during a special operation, two employees of The Ministry of Foreign Affairs were detained. They were suspected of abusing their administrative authority, of organizing and participating in contraband with excisable goods. For almost two months, 35-year-olds G.M. and A.N. from Sofia Security Police Department of the Ministry of Foreign Affairs were caught guarding shipments of contraband cigarettes in their free time. Both sergeants also were actively involved in distributing the goods in stores and storehouses all over the country, according to a statement issued by the ministry.

A much more serious case made headlines a few days later. More than 100 employees of the chief directorate for the Fight against Organized Crime made simultaneous checkups in hundreds of locations, inspecting, among others, 14 warehouses and offices of different companies. A day later, Hristo Grigorov, director of the Bulgarian Red Cross, was arrested. The checkups had been caused by a warning sign that food and clothes donations for disaster victims were illegally distributed on the free market. During the investigation it became clear that donations passing through the Bulgarian Red Cross were dedicated to the chief *mufti's* (Islamic scholar's) office in Bulgaria and later distributed to stores. The profit never reached the destitute people. Instead it went to a limited circle of people from the charity and chief *mufti*'s office. After a short period of time spent behind bars, Grigorov managed to keep his job. No one else was punished.

The next scandal that caused tension and angered the public opinion involved thefts from State Reserve and Wartime Stocks Agency. On Feb. 23, 2006, the Ministry of Disaster Management Policy broke the news that 200 million leva (US$130 million) worth of goods were missing from the agency. This included 65 million leva (US$42 million) worth of fuel and over 100 million leva (US$65 million) worth of wheat.

In view of the fact that the EU expects the Bulgarian authorities to adopt anti-corruption measures at the highest level of the power, on March 13, 2006, the government disclosed that 35 politicians charged with taking bribes were under investigation. Thirteen of them were former and current deputies in the National Assembly. The prosecutor's office introduced 35 indictments, according to a government report for implementation of criteria for joining the EU.

BULGARIA

March 6, 2006, was the date of the first coordinated meeting of the anti-corruption commissions in the National Assembly, Council of Ministers and Supreme Court Council. On the agenda was a report for violation of the law in management of the Kozlodui nuclear power plant. Under attack was Yordan Kostadinov, the former director of the plant and also a deputy in the current parliament. The scandal that followed proved the helplessness of this executive body in fighting corruption. Kostadinov is a member of Simeon II National Movement, one of the parties in the ruling coalition. The attempt of the socialists in the commission to investigate a representative of this party provoked united resistance on their part. The situation would be the same if Simeon II National Movement tried to attack the Bulgarian Socialist Party, or if either of them went against the third party in the coalition, the National Movement for Rights and Freedom, which represents the interests of the ethnic Turk population in Bulgaria. From all this we could draw the only conclusion that no disclosure of large dimensions should be expected in Bulgaria during the rule of the three-party coalition, which is in power until the country is scheduled to join the EU in January 2007.

Finally came good news. The court took on a case revealed in the BBC documentary "Buying the Games." Ivan Slavkov, the son-in-low of former dictator Todor Jivkov and chairman of the Bulgarian Olympic Committee, was suspended in August after being implicated in an alleged corruption scandal. Despite the evidence brought against Slavkov in the documentary, the D.A.'s office opened a case, not against

him, but against the BBC journalists, charging them with using a hidden camera, a practice that is not allowed by Bulgarian law.

Several days later, there came more good news. The
chief of Municipal Markets Co., Venelin Marinov, was arrested just five minutes after taking a bribe of in 200 leva
(US$139) marked bills. In a drawer of his desk, an additional
3,000 leva (US$2,000) were found, according to a source
from the Ministry of Internal Affairs.

His arrest gave enough courage to the traders, who had
experienced great problems with him, to come forth and
officially report the "fees" they had to pay to receive certain
trade locations in the market. The price for a good location in
the market, for one year, was 2,000 leva (US$1,300). If one
paid for more than one stand at the same time, a discount
was applied, and the total amount one had to pay was 1,000
leva (US$650) per year per stand. For stores or booths, the
required bribe varied between 5,000 leva (US$3,350) and
10,000 leva (US$6,500).

"I will not hesitate to lift the immunity of a magistrate
or a deputy if there are evidences they are corrupted," said
Boris Velchev, the newly elected chief prosecutor. So far
Velchev has proven himself as a trustworthy politician who
stands firmly on his position. In early April 2006, Velchev
withdrew the immunity of seven deputies who had broken the
law prior to and during their mandate.

The battle, though, will not be easy. According to
Tihomir Bezlov, a representative of Center for the Study of
Democracy, between 320 million and 370 million leva (up to

BULGARIA

US$240 million) was misused through public orders in 2005. 55 million leva (US$36 million) in bribes alone were paid to gain contracts for public orders during the past year. The average cost of the bribe is 7.4 percent of the total amount of the contract, according to data from a report prepared by the Center. Internal investigation, carried by an undercover employee working with traffic policemen, showed that five of seven representatives of power regularly take bribes while they are on duty.

On Sept. 25, 2006, the European Commission will issue its crucial report on progress made by Bulgaria and Romania. According to Franco Fratini, the European commissioner for justice, Bulgaria still has a chance to join the EU on Jan. 1, 2007.

It is true that corruption at the moment in Bulgaria is far behind the levels of 1990–2000, but it is still high for a state that is poised to become a member of the EU.

For an alternative perspective, read the critical peer review commentary on this notebook, part of the 2006 Global Integrity Report (www.globalintegrity.org).

Cambodia:
At a Crossroads
By Global Integrity*

Tan Monivann said his investment firm has no choice but to pay bribes to officials in the Cambodian government. Without doing so, he said, his business would suffer.

"Bribery is a habit that has become part of the culture, and if we don't pay bribes, our business' work will be delayed," said Monivann, vice president of the Mong Reththy Group. He noted that public ministries often refuse to return official documents until he pays "unofficial fees."

Monivann faults low civil servant salaries and the government's lack of formal procedures for processing paperwork for the corruption plaguing his country.

Cambodia lost 75 percent of its annual income taxes in 2005 because of corruption in the private sector, according to an Economic Institute of Cambodia (EIC) report released in July 2006. The report found that the private sector paid 1.37

* The author is a Cambodian journalist who reqested his/her name be witheheld, citing the potential threat of government recrimination.

trillion riels (US$330 million) in bribes in 2005. That amount represents about 50 percent of total governmental revenues for 2005. Only 25 percent of potential taxes were collected from businesses in 2005.

"The potential loss in the government revenue could reach (US)$400 million," the report concluded. "Small and medium enterprises and large enterprises pay unofficial fees to receive services and maintain good relations with public officials."

In fact, if corruption were eliminated, the government would have enough money to raise salaries of civil servants, according to the report. The average civil servant currently makes about 104,350 riels (US$25) a month. Without the lost revenue due to corruption, those salaries could increase to 417,400 riels (US$100) or 626,100 riels (US$150) a month.

In the private sector, corruption often occurs when public officials perform inspections, which the report characterized as nothing more than pretexts to demand money. In total, bribes represent between 1.8 and 4.1 percent of annual sales for businesses, depending on their size.

In an August 2006 public statement, Prime Minister Hun Sen strongly criticized the report, arguing that it exaggerated the level of corruption in Cambodia.

"If the government collected [income tax at] only 25 percent, the government would collapse," he said. "Can we believe that we lose 75 percent and collect only 25 percent? If a family gets 25 percent of their income, and 75 percent is used by the husband and children to gamble and use drugs, can the family survive and have enough rice to eat?"

Sen acknowledged that corruption exists, but said the EIC's report overstated the problem. "I would believe that we collected 70 percent and lost 30 percent," he said. "But 70 percent lost means that people in the whole country are thieves, and the private sector and the government officials are also thieves."

The government will fight illegal smuggling and corruption, Sen said. Sen disputed that the loss of revenue from corruption was the cause of low civil servant salaries. He blamed the delayed payment of the salaries—sometimes more than two months late—on ministers failing to make timely requests to the National Bank for the funds.

"Civil servants receive their salaries late, and it's not because the government doesn't have enough money at the National Bank," he said.

Private sector and public officials who were surveyed for the report said they believed that the four major causes of corruption in Cambodia are: the low salary of public officials, a lack of an effective anti-corruption mechanism, a culture of corruption and a lack of an independent and effective judiciary. Low salaries were listed as the primary reason for soliciting bribes.

Sen called the EIC's director, Sok Hach, an "ignorant scholar" and urged him to stop publicizing the report.

Sam Rainsy, head of the opposition Sam Rainsy Party, said the report was accurate and that the country would never develop if it did not take action to fight corruption.

"It's like being positive for AIDS. If we hide the disease and refuse treatment, we will die," he said.

CAMBODIA

He also blamed low teacher and civil servant salaries on the loss of national revenue caused by corruption.

The EIC's report came shortly after the World Bank in June accused the Cambodian government of corruption in some World Bank-financed projects. The World Bank said the government misused funds during the bidding process on 49.7 billion riels (US$11.9 million) worth of contracts for public works projects. It has asked the government to return part of that money, but so far, the government has refused. Only one major official - a member of one of the ruling party's coalition partners - has been arrested. No one from the ruling Cambodian People's Party has been charged.

In June, Hun Sen said the World Bank did not provide the government with enough evidence to substantiate its accusations.

"The World Bank cannot try the government without evidence, so we don't have to pay them back," Sen said.

Rainsy said the government has yet to conduct an adequate investigation.

"The government arrested only small officials, but the top government officials who are responsible are still at large," Rainsy said. "If we want to clean the house, we should clean it from top to bottom."

National Assembly member and Deputy Chairman of the Justice Commission Monh Saphan agreed with the EIC report, saying corruption exists in the private sector because of poor law enforcement, low civil servant salaries and the lack of anti-corruption regulations.

The government recently failed on its promise to adopt

an anti-corruption law by the end of June, which it had pledged to do during its annual meeting with international donors last March.

The government has written a draft version of the law, but it has yet to send it to the National Assembly for passage. The draft version of the anti-corruption law makes corruption a criminal offense; officials found guilty would face one to 15 years in prison, along with fines.

Under the law, the government would establish a commission charged with investigating corruption. The law would require all members of the government, National Assembly, military, police, civil service and judiciary to declare their assets upon assuming and leaving their positions.

National Assembly Finance and Banking Commission Chairman Cheam Yeap, member of the ruling Cambodian People's Party, said the government is trying to get the anti-corruption law up to international standards before it sends the legislation to the Assembly.

"The anti-corruption law will be adopted soon," he said. "We will punish corrupted officials. The anti-corruption law will provide a sword to the government and the court to prosecute corrupt officials. We will eradicate corruption in Cambodia."

Kurt A. MacLeod, Asia regional director of Pact, a nongovernmental organization working to combat corruption, said after the release of the EIC's report that the revenues the Cambodian government would gain by eliminating corruption could help the government expand the economy.

"It has the opportunity to become a beacon of light in

CAMBODIA

Asia, and at the forefront of economic growth. This is only possible if the Royal Government of Cambodia begins to take serious action on creating a clean Cambodia," MacLeod said.

"There is a high demand for a clean Cambodia," Macleod continued. "Cambodia is at a crossroads; the choice is clear. It is now up to the Royal Government of Cambodia and the citizens of this country to take action against corruption for the future of its citizens and children."

For an alternative perspective, read the critical peer review commentary on this notebook, part of the 2006 Global Integrity Report (www.globalintegrity.org).

Democratic Republic of Congo:
Who Watches the Watchers?

By Kazadi Mpoyi-Mutombo

Corruption has become a phenomenon in the Democratic Republic of Congo, leaving no part of national life untouched. It pervades society from the highest public offices to the most underprivileged citizens.

The Congolese economy was devastated by 30 years of dictatorship marked by corruption and nepotism, resulting in an annual per-capita income of about 42,000 francs (US$80). Following the assassination of President Laurent Kabila in 2001 and the succession of his son Joseph, an agency called the Commission of Repression of Economic Crimes was established. Unfortunately, the organization did not live up to its name: The French National Assembly adopted a law in March 2005 outlawing corruption.

Bribes have become necessary in order to obtain anything from the country's public servants, who resort to corruption because of their low pay-around 30,000 francs (US$55). A member of the National Observatory of Human Rights (ONDH—*Observatoire National des Droits de l'Homme*), an institution charged with defending human rights in the country, testified that he was asked in July 2006 to pay bribes to government officials at the Directorate-General of Migration to obtain permission to fly from Kinshasa to Inongo, a city located in the Maï-Ndombe district in the province of Bandundu.

The public tolerates this corruption because the authorities responsible for fighting corruption are widely perceived as corrupt themselves. In 2005, officials from the ministries of transportation, communications, foreign trade and mines were suspended of corruption following an incriminating report by the government's auditing agency. The ministers never appeared before a judge because of a pardon by President Joseph Kabila. Citizens invoke the Congolese proverb "the fish starts rotting at the head" to describe how corruption starts at the top.

But the public is not immune. A citizen who works with a state institution established to regulate the media said one day two traffic officers stopped him in Kinshasa and demanded to see his registration documents. The officers then told him his car violated emission standards. Although the employee explained that he had just tuned his engine and that he was late for an appointment at another government agency, the officers asked him to pay 8,400 francs (US$18). After paying 1,500 francs (US$3), they let him go.

In another example, a pastor went to register his church with the government, a procedure that generally costs 15,500 francs (US$30) for records and deposit, and 26,000 francs (US$50) for a state audit. The official handling his case charged him an extra 16,000 francs (US$31) for the registration documents, bypassing the audit altogether and promising to defend the pastor if he found himself the target of harassment by other officials. Similar stories of officials issuing licenses and registrations without the required tests or documentation abound. For example, driver's licenses are often issued for a price, despite the absence of vision or other health tests.

The Ministry of Foreign Affairs is not exempt from these practices. An investigation found that the list of bribes necessary to obtain a passport is long and expensive. First, one must pay 9,000 francs (US$20) to the ministry of justice for documentation of one's criminal record, then 62,000 francs (US$120) for other documents — all this above the "legal" price of 41,400 francs (US$80). Top ministry officials, who see their agents trolling outside the ministry building for passport-seekers, tolerate this practice. The Directorate General of Taxes is infamous for cutting deals in which businessmen pay less to the government in exchange for a fee to government agents and a promise that the agents will protect them from tax auditors.

The Commission of Ethics and Anti-Corruption (CELC—*Commission d'Ethique et de Lutte contre la Corruption*) says it approaches its task by "sensitizing" rather than "repressing" corruption. A CELC official said a May 2006 investigation on the pervasiveness of corruption in the country found that the Katanga province, where much ore is mined, is particularly bad. Smuggling and corruption have

D. R. CONGO

The Global Integrity Index:
How effective are the Democratic Republic of Congo's anti-corruption safeguards?

OVERALL RATING

Very Weak (44)

CATEGORY RATINGS

1) Civil Society, Public Information & Media — Very Weak (40)

2) Elections — Very Weak (57)

3) Government Accountability — Very Weak (32)

4) Administration & Civil Service — Very Weak (62)

5) Oversight & Regulation — Very Weak (62)

6) Anti-Corruption & Rule of Law — Very Weak (68)

(Scores range from 0 to 100)

The Global Integrity Index, through the Integrity Indicators, assesses the existence and effectiveness of national anti-corruption mechanisms. It does not measure corruption itself (which is nearly impossible). Instead, the Index analyzes the opposite of corruption: the institutions and practices that promote more accountable government and prevent, deter or punish corruption.

The Index is based on nearly 300 Integrity Indicators, discrete scores assigned by local experts using a consistent methodology and scoring criteria for each country. These results are then blindly peer reviewed at the local and international level to ensure consistency and accuracy.

All of the more than 11,000 Integrity Indicator scores that comprise the 2006 Index are published—along with extensive commentary, references and critical peer review comments and perspectives—in the annual Global Integrity Report.

For full results and downloadable datasets, see the Global Integrity website (www.globalintegrity.org).

prevented the residents of Katanga province from benefiting from its rich natural resources. The United Nations released a statement in 2003 saying that in light of the plundering of the Democratic Republic of Congo's resources, the government must finally break with corruption.

For an alternative perspective, read the critical peer review commentary on this notebook, part of the 2006 Global Integrity Report (www.globalintegrity.org).

Arab Republic of Egypt:
Wicked Collaboration

By Sameh Fawzy Henien

On Feb 3, 2006, Egyptians woke up to a great disaster:
The Al-Salam Boccaccio 98 ferry sank shortly after leaving
Saudi Arabia on its way to the Egyptian port of Safaga. Only
338 passengers survived out of 1,414 on board.

The parliamentary committee that investigated the
catastrophe found that the ferry's owner had failed to meet a
series of basic safety standards. The committee condemned
"wicked collaboration" between the shipping company and
some top government officials. The investigation indicated
that the circumstances of the accident "point to a hideous image of corruption in a utility related to people's lives".

This is not an unusual incident in the Arab Republic
of Egypt. Every day, Egyptian opposition and newspapers
—both official and private—break stories about corrupt
government officials. The high level of centralization, low pay
structure, deeply rooted bureaucracy and the political influence on that bureaucracy all contribute to the problem. Over

the last few years, high-profile corruption cases have resulted in lengthy trials, leading, in some incidents, to the conviction of several government officials. These have included a former minister of finance, a former head of the Customs Authority, a former governor of the Giza governorate, as well as some prominent bankers involved in corruption related to unpaid loans. Newspapers and laypeople also report cases for which no official action has been taken, so far.

In 2002 alone, as many as 48 high-ranking officials, including former cabinet ministers, provincial governors and members of parliament, were convicted of influence peddling, favoritism, profiteering and embezzlement. The current law regulating legal proceedings against cabinet ministers suspected of illegal activities dates back to the 1958-1961 Egyptian-Syrian union. The law, still in place in Egypt, has never been implemented.

The parliamentary elections in 2005 witnessed wide-scale cases of vote purchasing, as voters sold their votes in poor areas in return for 30 Egyptian pounds (US$5)—the price of one kilo of beef. The purchase price for a vote soared to 1,000 Eygptian pounds (US$175) in wealthy areas, especially in the Naser city constituency in Cairo.

In addition, Viagra pills, cigarettes stuffed with cannabis, mobile phones, clothes and food have been used to gain constituency in the elections.

In 2006, there was a campaign against former heads and chief editors of government newspapers and magazines. It has been proven that one of these editors, the head of Al-Ahram newspaper, has earned around 3 million Egyptian pounds

The Global Integrity Index:
How effective are Egypt's anti-corruption safeguards?

OVERALL RATING

Very Weak (57)

CATEGORY RATINGS

1) Civil Society, Public Information & Media — Very Weak (52)

2) Elections — Very Weak (58)

3) Government Accountability — Very Weak (39)

4) Administration & Civil Service — Weak (62)

5) Oversight & Regulation — Weak (62)

6) Anti-Corruption & Rule of Law — Weak (68)

(Scores range from 0 to 100)

The Global Integrity Index, through the Integrity Indicators, assesses the existence and effectiveness of national anti-corruption mechanisms. It does not measure corruption itself (which is nearly impossible). Instead, the Index analyzes the opposite of corruption: the institutions and practices that promote more accountable government and prevent, deter, or punish corruption.

The Index is based on nearly 300 Integrity Indicators, discrete scores assigned by local experts using a consistent methodology and scoring criteria for each country. These results are then blindly peer reviewed at the local and international level to ensure consistency and accuracy.

All of the more than 11,000 Integrity Indicator scores that comprise the 2006 Index are published—along with extensive commentary, references and critical peer review comments and perspectives—in the annual Global Integrity Report.

For full results and downloadable datasets, see the Global Integrity website (www.globalintegrity.org).

(US$525,854) per month; more than the combined monthly salaries of 1,500 journalists.

Unfortunately Egyptians are accustomed to these kinds of public crimes, which cost lives, kill hopes and perpetuate depression. Corruption is not only a crime, but also a basic source of public despair. It makes people's lives miserable and their futures bleak.

In Egypt, corruption has been systematically embedded into daily life. People have to bribe public employees to get illegal permits and public goods. Even services to which people are lawfully entitled aren't accessible without "lubricating" the government's bureaucratic machine with money.

Public employees, in turn, are usually rent-seeking, looking for small cash tips from people to compensate the pitiful salaries they get. When my father passed away, I went to the special court where people obtain their "inheritance declaration" after a relative dies. I was asked by the lawyer to give the court clerk five Egyptian pounds (US$0.88) to receive my father's declaration without delay. I resisted at first, but conceded after I found everybody else bribing the secretary, who ends up collecting no less than 250 pounds (US$44) a day—almost as much as his official monthly salary. While not a university graduate, the man's monthly income exceeds the salary of someone who holds a Ph.D. and works in a government organization.

It also is common practice to pay civil clerks to move files ahead of other cases, speeding up the legal process.

There are four major governmental areas that are most associated with corruption: government purchases, customs

EGYPT

and taxes, jobs recruitment and local administration.

Dr. Zakareya Azmy, the president's chief of staff and a prominent parliamentarian, describes local administration as "sinking up to its ears in corruption." The local authorities enjoy enormous power over people's day-to-day lives. They license shops, monitor markets and issue permits for erecting new buildings or repairing existing ones. Generally speaking, it is difficult to get the required license for any of these activities without paying the local employees, who sometimes constitute networks based on patronage distribution. If a contractor wishes to make a building that exceeds the legal height limits, he has to pay a bribe of around 100,000 Egyptian pounds (US$17,528). The figure may decrease to half if he only wants to illegally install electricity or a clean water system in the building.

Local authorities benefit from the growth of the informal labor sector. In a country like Egypt, where around 5 million people work in this underground economy, the relationship between these workers and local authorities is crucial.

Consider this: Young street traders often sell their goods without authorization. They buy cheap Chinese imported commodities from wholesale merchants and sell them to the public in the crowded streets. Not only are these merchants tax evaders, to a certain extent they are cheaters, using every means to deceive low-class consumers who live in the suburbs of Cairo or visit the capital to buy cheap commodities. These sellers have to bribe the employees of the local authorities to let them illegally occupy the streets. However, due to the local authorities' rampant corruption, government inspectors sporadically roam streets to chase away illegal vendors.

In these situations, public employees sustain their interests and protect themselves, so the illegal vendors have to be vigilant and build their own safety network. They recruit young people scattered in the streets to quickly send warning in case of danger. During sudden official inspection campaigns, the vendors collect and pack their wares and hide, often in the small living rooms that belong to nearby buildings' guards, who charge a small amount of money in return.

The traffic is another example of daily corruption. If you want to avoid a harsh violation penalty, you can usually bribe the low-ranking street policemen 10 or 20 pounds (US$1.75 or US$3.50).

It is normal for small vans to break traffic laws in the streets of metropolitan Cairo. These vans are sometimes driven by underage, unlicensed drivers. Some analysts believe that these fleets of vans are covertly run by high-level bureaucratic officials in administrative and security positions who safeguard the vans' drivers and disregard all committed violations.

In Egypt, there are many watchdog organizations that cost a lot, but don't produce a clear outcome. Their jurisdictions overlap and their functions usually depend on the political will. Although the laws governing these monitoring organizations do not require secrecy, their periodic reports tend to be difficult to access. Politicians (including People's Assembly members), journalists, academics and laypeople find it difficult to obtain these reports for accurate informa-

EGYPT

tion about the drain of public resources.

Corruption has become a myth in a society like Egypt: People talk a lot about it, while accurate information relating to the phenomenon is rare.

For an alternative perspective, read the critical peer review commentary on this notebook, part of the 2006 Global Integrity Report (www.globalintegrity.org).

Ethiopia:
Early Education

By Tamrat G. Giorgis

The first time I heard about corruption, I was an elementary school student. The news on the state media radio was too loud and persistent, and the dumbfounded reaction of those around me too strong to forget my first exposure to a phenomenon that has become a subject of international concern today.

It was June 1985: Tesfaye Tikue, head of finance at a state farm, was convicted of embezzling 80,018 Ethiopian birr (US$40,000) over five years beginning in 1978.

The special tribunal established by the military government to try corruption cases decided that Tesfaye should not only pay back the money plus a 3,000 birr (US$343) penalty, but serve 13 years in prison without parole.

This affair came at the height of Ethiopia's first attempt to institutionalize the fight against widespread corruption. It became the effort's poster child. In a country where a top general's salary was not more than 4,371 birr (US$500), people could hardly contain their disbelief that anyone could siphon off such a huge sum of money.

Until then, corruption was perceived as perfectly normal in Ethiopia, but limited to petty gifts to the bureaucracy or in the courts.

"Offering and receiving bribes and various forms of corruption on the one hand, and the disposition of public functions on a discretionary basis by favoring clients and supplicants on the other, were viewed as normal," concluded a 2001 survey conducted by the Institute of Educational Research of the Addis Abeba University.

The Civil Service Agency, created by Emperor Hailesellasies' government in 1942, was tasked with various administrative regulatory roles, including control of the traditional practice of accepting bribes. Once the public took to the streets protesting the corrupt practices of his ministers, however, corruption became a fact of the Ethiopian social fabric, for both rulers and the ruled.

Tesfaye's story was significant not only because it was one of the 3,487 cases the special tribunal tried in the mid-1980s, but also because the verdict came a year after the military government established the first institution solely responsible for fighting corruption. The Workers' Committee for Control (WCC) was created in 1984 with the authority to receive whistleblower tips and public complaints, as well as investigate and prosecute culprits.

Beyond Tesfaye, however, it was hardly a successful venture. No other significant case emerged before the collapse of the military regime in 1991. Many believe this was because corruption grew too deep a root during this period: investigators simply had run out of steam by the time the WCC imploded, along with the government that created it.

The Ethiopian public had to wait 20 years before another corruption case was brought to a court of law, again of astounding proportions. Abate Kisho, then president of the regional administration in southern Ethiopia, and Bitew Belay, a senior cadre of the ruling party assigned to the same region, were convicted by the Federal High Court for abuse of office in connection with contracts awarded to their "friends in the private sector."

Abate and Bitew were accused of violating the regional state's procurement directives when they placed orders to buy equipment worth 74.1 million Birr (US$15 million) for the bureaus of Works and Urban Development, and Natural Resources Development and Environmental Protection. The first ruling found the defendants guilty and passed a six-year prison sentence for Abate and Bitew, who were tried in absentia but never returned to the country, and two years for Negussie, though an appeal ended up increasing his sentence.

The most high profile case waged in Ethiopia in the name of fighting corruption involved the former prime minister, and later defense minister, Tamrat Layne. He is serving an 18-year jail sentence after the federal high court found him guilty of stashing a state fund worth 16 million dollars in his personal Swiss bank account.

The new government created a new watchdog agency in 2001 called the Federal Ethics and Anticorruption

ETHIOPIA

The Global Integrity Index:
How effective are Ethiopia's anti-corruption safeguards?

OVERALL RATING
Moderate (77)

CATEGORY RATINGS

1) Civil Society, Public Information & Media — Moderate (72)

2) Elections — Very Weak (56)

3) Government Accountability — Weak (69)

4) Administration & Civil Service — Strong (87)

5) Oversight & Regulation — Strong (88)

6) Anti-Corruption & Rule of Law — Strong (89)

(Scores range from 0 to 100)

The Global Integrity Index, through the Integrity Indicators, assesses the existence and effectiveness of national anti-corruption mechanisms. It does not measure corruption itself (which is nearly impossible). Instead, the Index analyzes the opposite of corruption: the institutions and practices that promote more accountable government and prevent, deter or punish corruption.

The Index is based on nearly 300 Integrity Indicators, discrete scores assigned by local experts using a consistent methodology and scoring criteria for each country. These results are then blindly peer reviewed at the local and international level to ensure consistency and accuracy.

All of the more than 11,000 Integrity Indicator scores that comprise the 2006 Index are published—along with extensive commentary, references and critical peer review comments and perspectives—in the annual Global Integrity Report.

For full results and downloadable datasets, see the Global Integrity website (www.globalintegrity.org).

Commission. It was followed by similar agencies in the regional states and the appointment of ethics officers in every state organization.

Despite these recent developments, corruption in today's Ethiopia spreads unabated. Public opinion suggests that Ethiopia is among worst in the world. Surveys compiled by Transparency International in 2005 ranked Ethiopia 137th out of 159 nations polled, alongside countries such as Cameroon, Liberia, Iraq, Azerbaijan, Uzbekistan and Indonesia.

A businessman once cynically described Ethiopia as the land of "10 percent," meaning hardly anything can be accomplished without adding this amount as a kickback.

"Of late, going through [a transaction] without paying a bribe in Ethiopia is seen as an achievement by peers," wrote Kebour Ghenna, former president of the Addis Abeba Chamber of Commerce, and now director of Initiative Africa, a non-government organization.

His is not an isolated view. A 2001 survey conducted by the Institute of Educational Research on 600 firms across the regional states revealed that 78.5 percent believed corruption in the public sector negatively influenced their operations and growth, placing public sector corruption second only to unemployment in Ethiopia's 18 largest socio-economic problems.

More recently, nearly 40 percent of small and medium enterprises surveyed in 2005 by the World Bank Institute named corruption as one of the three major challenges to successfully running their businesses, along with problems in

ETHIOPIA

tax administration and access to land.

Corruption has reached a disastrous juncture, according to a retired civil servant with over 40 years of service spanning three regimes.

"Despite the creation of a commission, we haven't seen anything more than propaganda and educational materials," he said over a lunch hosted by the French Ambassador to Ethiopia.

He was partly referring to an evening airtime slot on national TV that attempts to educate the public on how corruption impoverishes society. According to Brehanu Assefa, a senior public relations advisor to the Commission, the Commission has distributed 75,000 magazines, 48,000 posters, 265,000 brochures and 120,000 fliers in the five years since its establishment, in addition to providing training to 267 federal offices and enterprises. Since its inception, prosecutors at the Commission have prosecuted 450 cases, of which 55 ended in convictions. There are now over 110 cases pending at the courts; the Commission received over 1,000 tips from the public last year and will prosecute 565 suspects, according to its chief, Ali Sulaiman.

But despite all these fliers, figures and pending cases, fighting corruption is widely perceived as an instrument employed by the ruling party to prosecute its political opponents.

The last minute amendment of the anticorruption bill hardly helped to persuade the public otherwise. Parliament amended the bill in 2001, one day after its ratification (a legislative speed unrivaled in Ethiopian history) after a court released Seyee Abraha on bail. Seyee was a senior politician within the ruling coalition who dissented from his colleagues during the major crises that followed the end of the bloody Ethio-Eritrean war. The amendment effectively denied bail to corruption defendants. Seyee was arrested again, together with his brothers and a sister, on charges of abusing his high office by enriching family members, a charge he is still fighting in the Supreme Court from prison.

At about the same time, state security services arrested several top businesspeople, officials of the state privatization agency and 42 staff members of the state-owned Commercial Bank of Ethiopia (CBE), including its former chief, Tilahun Abay.

The bankers and state workers were charged with either advancing loans to the accused businesspeople, violating the Bank's lending policies or selling state-owned enterprises against privatization regulation. These cases are pending before the courts five years after first emerging.

After this inauspicious start, the state's drive to fight corruption hasn't quite recovered its credibility.

Now corruption has become so pervasive that it is no longer limited to the public sector. "Ten percent kickback" has become a keyword for private firms that award procurement or project contracts to other private companies. Kebour Ghenna described this as "private-to-private" corruption.

"The fact that people talk less about it, as compared to the private-to-public corruption, may have led many outside the business world to think it is not significant," Kebour wrote in the World Bank magazine.

ETHIOPIA

In fact, many believe private-to-private corruption is affecting their lives. According to the survey by the Institute of Educational Research, nearly 40 percent of the 600 firms surveyed said corruption in the private sector impedes their operations and ability to grow.

For an alternative perspective, read the critical peer review commentary on this notebook, part of the 2006 Global Integrity Report (www.globalintegrity.org).

Georgia:
Mikhail the Great

By Daria Vaisman

Though Georgian President Mikhail Saakashvili counts controversial Turkish reformer Kemal Ataturk as a role model, his presidency more closely resembles that of a leader from Georgia's northern neighbor: Catherine the Great, the "enlightened despot" who famously shoved Russia into the 18th century with a combination of "legislomania" and liberal reforms borrowed from Europe.

Georgia too has become a case study for the impact of a strong leader on a weak state. Whether a dominant executive power is necessary to quickly reform a dying and corrupt government or presages authoritarianism is a topic frequently debated in Tbilisi.

Yet no one here doubts that Georgia is better off now than when Saakashvili took over in 2003. During that year's Rose Revolution, when Saakashvili replaced Eduard Shevardnadze, Georgia was a failed state, ranking alongside Bangladesh and Nigeria as one of the most corrupt in the world. Its largest export was scrap metal.

Today, Georgia has become the darling of international organizations and a key component of an increasingly Russophobe U.S. policy—a happy position that is as much the result of geopolitics as successful reform at home. According to a recent World Bank report, Georgia is this year's transitional-country success story, having slashed corruption more than any other country in Europe and Central Asia. Its GDP continues to grow at a respectable 7 to 8 percent despite a Russian ban on Georgian wine and water—its largest exports—and a worryingly high inflation rate.

Perceptions have changed along with the numbers. "Corruption is not the rule anymore: You're no longer expected to be corrupt," said Georgian political scientist Gia Nodia. Police who once shook down drivers on invented offenses now drive amiably by in new cars. Smart students, previously unable to get into universities because they couldn't afford the bribes, now choose their school by taking a standardized test. Businesses that once hid revenue to avoid paying taxes now pay regularly, allowing the Finance Ministry to draft longer-term budgets. Corrupt officials have been fired and replaced, unused infrastructure privatized, dilapidated streets repaved and shops and cafes established in the city's center. Not surprisingly, tourism is at its highest level since Georgia's independence in 1992.

So why are so many Georgians complaining? To begin with, life is more expensive. Disposable income has dropped despite a slight increase in salaries because of a much higher increase in the price of consumer goods. More than half of the population outside Tbilisi lives under the poverty line (defined by the World Bank as US$2 a day, roughly equivalent to three lari), and up to a third of the population in Tbilisi is unemployed.

Another explanation is the normal letdown following the euphoria of the revolution. According to the 2004 Transparency International Global Corruption Barometer, 60 percent of Georgians expected corruption to decrease during the next three years—the biggest positive change in corruption perceptions worldwide. Only 38 percent said they believed the same one year later, a 22 percent drop. But a comparison of which institutions Georgians consider corrupt may indicate positive change. The police force, ranked Georgia's most corrupt institution in 2004, dropped in 2005 to 9th place out of 15. The Tax Administration, ranked the second most corrupt institution in 2004, placed fourth the following year.

Both the Interior and Finance ministries (police and taxes) were completely overhauled by the Georgian government during 2004 and 2005, demonstrating the government's ability to rout sector-specific corruption—or at least create that impression. The remaining problems are most obvious in the health sector and judiciary, neither of which have been subjected to systemic reform. However, the educational system has been successful in turning a bribe-riddled university entrance process into a merit-based one.

However the elite, well-educated "NGO class"—the intellectual core of Shevardnadze-era Georgia that worked closely with Saakashvili during the revolution—worry that the government is reforming haphazardly without developing

GEORGIA

The Global Integrity Index:
How effective are Georgia's anti-corruption safeguards?

OVERALL RATING

Moderate (78)

CATEGORY RATINGS

1) Civil Society, Public Information & Media — Moderate (79)

2) Elections — Moderate (78)

3) Government Accountability — Moderate (78)

4) Administration & Civil Service — Weak (67)

5) Oversight & Regulation — Strong (81)

6) Anti-Corruption & Rule of Law — Strong (85)

(Scores range from 0 to 100)

The Global Integrity Index, through the Integrity Indicators, assesses the existence and effectiveness of national anti-corruption mechanisms. It does not measure corruption itself (which is nearly impossible). Instead, the Index analyzes the opposite of corruption: the institutions and practices that promote more accountable government and prevent, deter or punish corruption.

The Index is based on nearly 300 Integrity Indicators, discrete scores assigned by local experts using a consistent methodology and scoring criteria for each country. These results are then blindly peer reviewed at the local and international level to ensure consistency and accuracy.

All of the more than 11,000 Integrity Indicator scores that comprise the 2006 Index are published—along with extensive commentary, references and critical peer review comments and perspectives—in the annual Global Integrity Report.

For full results and downloadable datasets, see the Global Integrity website (www.globalintegrity.org).

institutions that will last beyond Saakshvili's tenure. They also fear that the additional powers granted the executive branch by the legislature has eroded the political system's checks and balances.

The government argues it is taking necessary steps to keep reforms moving at the proper clip. A feeling pervades that time is limited, fueled in many ways by the perception that Russia is waiting in the wings to countermand Georgia's success, as it did with Ukraine.

Nodia refers to the current style of government as "authoritarian modernization lite," or what would have happened if Ataturk or Catherine the Great were regularly monitored by the European Union and NATO (which Georgia very much hopes to join). The World Bank stated it more succinctly in a 2006 anti-corruption report: "Strong leadership yields results."

The divide between the government and the "NGO class" is widening. Dato Darchiashvili, head of the Open Society Institute's Georgia office, calls it a "polarization from within." Being tagged "pro-government" by a member of the NGO crowd is tantamount to an attack, surprising because most influential government officials started their careers at NGOs.

But with a couple of exceptions, particularly regarding human rights, the disgruntled NGO heads I spoke with criticized the government's style—sweeping, quick, and done behind closed doors—rather than its reforms. Tamuna Karosanidze, head of Transparency International Georgia, complains that NGOs and outside experts are not consulted

GEORGIA

in the drafting of new legislation. Zurab Burduli, executive director of the Georgian Young Lawyers Association (GYLA), says the Parliament now functions as a glorified notary. Republican Party opposition leader Tina Khidasheli points out that the criminal procedures code introduced by the current government changed 28 times. Laws are changed to fit a precedent, she said, rather than precedents set to form law. One bank in Georgia lists "government actions that are not predictable" under their force majeure clause, usually reserved for "acts of God" such as floods and earthquakes.

Saakashvili is often called a PR president, but it is "one-sided PR," said Burduli. Shows, festivals and fireworks displays function more as bread and circuses than public forums. Burduli claimed that of a special 60 million lari (US$3.5 million) presidential fund, only 4,000 lari (US$2,300) went to its intended source: The rest went to PR events. When the government was criticized for the fund, it introduced a law in 2006 eliminating any mention of the fund's purpose from the budget.

Ramishvili said he thinks the NGOs are the problem. "The government is working at a supersonic speed and civil society is still working at a Shevardnadze speed," he said. As for the opposition, "they just boycott everything. Democracy can't function in that mode."

Regarding corruption, however, even the most vehement opposition figure concedes that today's Georgia is a dramatic improvement over its former self. The biggest change is that, by all accounts, the constant low-level bribes demanded for every basic function—from getting a passport to driving a car —has stopped.

Following implementation of the 2004 tax code, which replaced a progressive income tax with a flat tax of 12 percent and simplified tax administration, the percentage of firms reporting frequent bribery of tax officials fell from 44 to 11 percent between 2002 and 2005 in a World Bank survey—by far the most significant drop of any country. Collection rates have also improved considerably to include roughly 60 percent of the population.

Though low-level corruption is down, uncorroborated stories persist of higher "elite corruption," such as kickbacks for procurement and privatization deals. Khidasheli said she has seen procurement contracts issued directly to government officials' relatives. There is no doubt that kickbacks occur, as do all forms of corruption, but as American Chamber of Commerce president Fady Asly said, the difference between Georgia now and Georgia then is the difference between Nigeria and France.

"Effects are king," said Nodia. And so, for now, is Saakashvili.

For an alternative perspective, read the critical peer review commentary on this notebook, part of the 2006 Global Integrity Report (www.globalintegrity.org).

GEORGIA

Ghana:
2,000 Kilograms of Outrage
By Sarah Akrofi-Quarcoo

Last year, surveys by Transparency International showed that more people in Ghana believe the country has a corruption problem. Upon hearing this news, I was jubilant. For me, the increasingly negative views showed that our society is cleaning up. A change in perception implies a change in attitude. Ghana was saying no to *"Abaayenii"*—a Ga expression that literally means "man must chop."

The culture of the "chop," the need to eat, is still pervasive in Ghana. But with increasing frequency, there are people willing to decry the status quo and expose corruption.

As I write this report, a committee of inquiry set up by the Interior Ministry is sitting on one of the country's biggest scandals ever. It is a case of alleged bribery and drug trafficking; at its core are the Ghana Police service and other security agencies.

The scandal revolves around the inquiry committee's investigation of a May 2006 raid of an impounded vessel, the

MV Benjamin. On board were 2,000 kilograms of cocaine that allegedly belonged to a Venezuelan living in Ghana. The massive drug bust has sprawled into a political scandal, as it suggests that a number of high-ranking police officials are collaborating with the drug barons.

The director general of police operations has been suspended, on the orders of the Interior Ministry, after the discovery of a tape that revealed his meeting with four suspected drug traffickers. The secretly recorded tape was passed from a high-ranking official of the Food and Drugs Board to the head of state and now, figuratively, hangs around the director general's neck.

The scandal continues. Immigration officials, when questioned, failed to produce documents regarding the travel history of some South Americans linked to case. A star witness for the committee claims she received 2.8 billion cedis (US$300,000) from the Venezuelan. The money, she says, was intended to bribe the police.

In some countries, such a public disgrace would be unmentionable. But the press, radio and TV have been awash with stories on the scandal. Thanks to a pluralistic environment, a more vibrant media is up to the task of providing up-to-date information and engendering public discussion on the committee's proceedings, which have so far been open to the press. However, media accountability for the quality of reporting has come under intense public scrutiny as some newspapers have begun to politicize the issue.

People I interviewed about the drug scandal have called for wholesale resignations of the inspector general of police

GHANA

The Global Integrity Index:
How effective are Ghana's anti-corruption safeguards?

OVERALL RATING
Moderate (78)

CATEGORY RATINGS

1) Civil Society, Public Information & Media — Moderate (76)

2) Elections — Stong (81)

3) Government Accountability — Moderate (73)

4) Administration & Civil Service — Weak (63)

5) Oversight & Regulation — Very Strong (94)

6) Anti-Corruption & Rule of Law — Strong (83)

(Scores range from 0 to 100)

The Global Integrity Index, through the Integrity Indicators, assesses the existence and effectiveness of national anti-corruption mechanisms. It does not measure corruption itself (which is nearly impossible). Instead, the Index analyzes the opposite of corruption: the institutions and practices that promote more accountable government and prevent, deter or punish corruption.

The Index is based on nearly 300 Integrity Indicators, discrete scores assigned by local experts using a consistent methodology and scoring criteria for each country. These results are then blindly peer reviewed at the local and international level to ensure consistency and accuracy.

All of the more than 11,000 Integrity Indicator scores that comprise the 2006 Index are published—along with extensive commentary, references and critical peer review comments and perspectives—in the annual Global Integrity Report.

For full results and downloadable datasets, see the Global Integrity website (www.globalintegrity.org).

(IGP) and all those connected to the crime. Their position has resonated in radio phone-in programs across the country. Callers were outraged over news reports that the IGP and one of the drug barons have been friends for more than 20 years.

Long before this scandal broke out, public perception of the police and corruption has been generally negative. The police have often been openly condemned in the media, and in conversations on the street for taking bribes from motorists, during vehicle registration and when handling court cases—events seen as "eating places" by some officers. Not surprisingly, the police topped a list of negatively viewed organizations in a 2005 Ghana Integrity Initiative (GII) study.

In a recent scandal, a police prosecutor plotted with the accused's counsel, allegedly accepting bribes to tamper with a rape case he was handling. The prosecutor, as reported by The Mirror, gave the victim and her mother the wrong date for the court hearing and managed to secure bail for the accused. In this case, Nana Oye Lithur, a human rights lawyer, intervened and exposed a plot that otherwise would have succeeded.

Undoubtedly, the police are not the only ones who "chop" in Ghana. In the case above, the accused reportedly bribed not only the prosecutor, but also two uncles of the victim.

The average Ghanaian believes *"Obiara didi wo ni edzuma hu,"* meaning that all people "chop" around their place of work. That is how Ghanaians are able to live despite poor salaries and working conditions; the average Ghanaian

GHANA

is paid about 9200 cedi (US$1) a day. In a public opinion survey published by GII in 2005, 70 percent of respondents admitted they had "been involved in bribery and corruption either as victims or perpetrators and accept the practice as normal."

The police are not the only institution with a reputation problem; the GII report also listed the Ministry of Education, the Judiciary Service, Public/Civil Service, Ministry of Health, Customs, Excise and Preventive Service and the Immigration Service among the least trusted organizations. A report by the Public Affairs Committee of Parliament named the Ministries of Education and Health as engaging in an array of corrupt practices including embezzlement, payments not supported by vouchers, vouchers not presented for audit, non-retirement of advances, unearned salaries, items not routed through accredited stores and payment of unearned salaries to officers.

The report also cited the Value Added Tax Services, Ghana's internal revenue service, for failing to collect taxes, and the Customs Excise and Preventative Service for failing to collect annual warehouse renewal fees.

There is no empirical evidence to indicate how much money public officers collect through bribes. One can get an indication, however, through personal stories of victims. My friend Catherine told me she paid a bribe of 15 million cedis (US$1,630) to someone connected to a customs official at the harbor, in order to facilitate the clearance of a container of goods she imported for sale. Despite the bribe, no receipt was issued for the transaction. She forgot that there were other customs and road traffic officials on the route to her destination, many of whom cashed in on the fact that she had no official documents covering the goods.

I spoke with Florence Dennis, executive secretary of the Ghana Anti-Corruption Committee, about corruption in Ghana. She said she believes the country is improving. Dennis argued that Ghanaians perceive corruption to be rising because of the intense media spotlight on the issue. The Freedom of Information Bill "when passed, will further empower the media to expose wrongdoing," she said.

Ghanaian journalists can take some pride in their recent record. They exposed what became known as the "Hotel Kufour Saga" that lead to the investigation of the president by the Commission on Human Rights and Administrative Justice (CHRAJ).

In another case, the media dug up a case of impropriety involving Dr. Richard Anane, then the Minister of Health, who later appeared before the CHRAJ. It is risky to generalize from the two instances and argue that the government's openness and accountability are improving. There is no doubt, however, that the media is a positive force in the fight to hold government accountable.

The government itself has also made efforts. The Whistleblower Law was passed in August 2006. Currently before Parliament is a new bill—the Proceeds of Crime Bill—aimed at empowering the security agencies to investigate and compel people to declare their sources of income and how they have acquired their property. Apart from exposing corruption among public officers, the proposed law is expected to

GHANA

bring about more openness and accountability to all sectors.

The political will to fight corruption has been clearly declared by the ruling government. Media and common citizens are likewise growing impatient with the culture of the "chop." Translating this will into action, however, remains a challenge.

For an alternative perspective, read the critical peer review commentary on this notebook, part of the 2006 Global Integrity Report (www.globalintegrity.org).

India:
Rules of the Road

By Ritu Sarin

These reminders keep cropping up, and it isn't a coincidence. As a reporter and a right-minded citizen, I have never handled a bribe or paid for information. But all around me, incidents keep reminding me of how widespread corruption is in the bustling Indian capital, where outside every government office, the Central Vigilance Commission (CVC) has hung notices reminding citizens that paying bribes is a crime.

First, a close family friend recently confessed he had, through a back channel, paid a hefty bribe of 689,235 rupees (US$15,000) to a district judge for settling a property dispute between him and the Delhi Development Authority (DDA).

My friend won the case, but the DDA challenged the order in the Delhi High Court. Having paid up once, my friend realized a second bribe must now be paid, this time to a High Court judge.

Then, just a few days ago, my driver called me very distressed late at night. He was seeking my help in bailing out his brother. The brother, also a driver, had knocked down a cyclist. The cyclist had sustained head injuries, and the brother was now in a police custody. I said I would look into the matter the following day.

The next morning, my driver nonchalantly informed me that his brother was back on duty. The police had demanded a bribe of 10,000 rupees (US$215) to avoid a formal complaint, but they had settled at 4,000 rupees (US$86). That is roughly the equivalent to a driver's monthly salary.

More unwritten rules of the road came my way while having breakfast at a neighbor's house. Her teenage son had just received his driver's license and was being advised by his mother about how to handle the traffic police, omnipresent on Delhi roads.

"Quietly hand over 100 rupees (US$2) to the constable. Otherwise, they will send you a *challan* (traffic citation) at home." The boy acquiesced. It was his first willing lesson on getting the better of the authorities in Delhi.

A property dispute, a road accident or a brush with the traffic police—these are instances of how people in my immediate circle recently resorted to paying bribes, and without much compunction. Over the years, despite several massive corruption scams being exposed, the malaise of corruption has festered. With more than a billion people, roughly a quarter of whom live in poverty, fighting high-level and petty corruption is a huge administrative and social problem.

In October 2005, Transparency International India (TII) tried to put a figure on the spread of the country's corruption problem.

The corruption study polled 14,000 respondents, 62 percent of whom admitted they had first-hand experience of paying bribes to access public services. Hardly 10 percent of the respondents said they felt corruption was on the decline. The report estimated the total sum of bribes paid to access public services at more than 208 billon rupees (US$4.5 billion).

The police topped the services accounting for the most bribes being paid, followed by the lower judiciary, land administration, government hospitals and schools. The corruption survey showed, for instance, that bribes were routinely paid for gaining admission to schools or to receive diagnostic services in a public hospital.

According to former Naval Chief Admiral R. H. Tahiliani, chairman of Transparency International India, the 2005 report reveals the disparity in corruption patterns in developed and developing countries.

"In the United States, the average citizen may not be affected by corruption. But in India, corruption is rampant at the grass-root level, since citizens have to pay bribes for services they are entitled to. Corruption everyday affects the poorest of the poor," he said.

Adding to this burden is the distressing frequency with which corruption has been exposed in several of the Government's poverty alleviation programs.

A recent World Bank study exposed endemic corruption in the disbursement of bank credit to farmers in states like Andhra Pradesh, where scores of farmers have committed suicide due to crippling debt. The study pegged the going bribe rate at 6.5 percent of the value of the approved loans.

INDIA

The Global Integrity Index:
How effective are India's anti-corruption safeguards?

OVERALL RATING

Moderate (75)

CATEGORY RATINGS

1) Civil Society, Public Information & Media — Moderate (75)

2) Elections — Moderate (78)

3) Government Accountability — Weak (68)

4) Administration & Civil Service — Moderate (75)

5) Oversight & Regulation — Weak (70)

6) Anti-Corruption & Rule of Law — Strong (83)

(Scores range from 0 to 100)

The Global Integrity Index, through the Integrity Indicators, assesses the existence and effectiveness of national anti-corruption mechanisms. It does not measure corruption itself (which is nearly impossible). Instead, the Index analyzes the opposite of corruption: the institutions and practices that promote more accountable government and prevent, deter or punish corruption.

The Index is based on nearly 300 Integrity Indicators, discrete scores assigned by local experts using a consistent methodology and scoring criteria for each country. These results are then blindly peer reviewed at the local and international level to ensure consistency and accuracy.

All of the more than 11,000 Integrity Indicator scores that comprise the 2006 Index are published—along with extensive commentary, references and critical peer review comments and perspectives—in the annual Global Integrity Report.

For full results and downloadable datasets, see the Global Integrity website (www.globalintegrity.org).

Before this, corruption scams have been unearthed
in the distribution of grain under the Public Distribution
Scheme (PDS), even in Delhi. As a result, the Supreme Court
in July 2005 asked the Delhi Government to publish all PDS
data on its website.

The Supreme Court's ruling was only a reiteration of
TII's findings, which said that Delhi's PDS was the second
most corrupt after that of Bihar, where it has been suggested
that 64 percent of grain meant for citizens living in poverty
was pilfered and sold in the open market. Last year in Bihar,
more than 165 million rupees (US$3.6 million) intended for
flood relief just disappeared.

With an increasingly activist judiciary and a combative
press, corruption scandals abound and often overlap. Consider some of the major scams exposed this year:

In December 2005, a sting operation conducted by a TV
channel caught 11 members of Parliament accepting bribes
for asking questions in Parliament. All the MPs involved in
the "cash-for-query" scandal were expelled from Parliament.

Shortly afterwards, a similar undercover operation exposed MPs demanding as much as a 45 percent commission
for allotting projects to fake companies from their annual
development funds. These MPs have since been suspended.

Three senior officials working on the India-U.S. cyber
security forum were arrested on charges of espionage. The evidence has revealed that one of them received 551,388 rupees
(US$12,000) for selling secrets to an American diplomat.

Following a Public Interest Litigation filed in the Delhi
High Court, municipal authorities submitted a list of 18,000

INDIA

unauthorized residential and commercial properties in the capital, which are now being demolished (the list of owners included several politicians). When the demolition drive began, several owners admitted they had paid bribes for the illegal construction.

Today, even the government's corruption-busters admit it may take years, even decades, for any cleansing drive to yield tangible results.

"Corruption is not declining and this is also because fighting corruption cannot only be a law enforcement issue. The [Central Bureau of Investigation] deals with cases of corruption among central government employees, while all projects dealing with poverty alleviation, development and infrastructure are monitored by state governments," said Vijay Shankar, Director of the Central Bureau of Investigation (CBI), India's premier anti-corruption bureau,

Parliament was recently informed that the CBI was waiting for authorization to prosecute 91 government officials, mostly from the Ministry of Finance.

"A positive aspect is that courts have taken some stringent measures to expose corruption and the government has also initiated useful administrative reforms," Shankar added. "But the fact remains that politicizing corruption suits everyone and the polity must now ensure it has one view on corruption."

That, unfortunately, remains an elusive ideal for an India in the grips of the politics of victimization, where each political regime exposes the graft or corruption of its predecessors, especially in cases of major purchases and defense deals.

Also, there are two crucial pieces of legislation that successive governments have avoided introducing. The first is the Lok Pal Bill, aimed at preventing corruption in high political offices, which has been in the works for more than three decades and has been again put on hold by the present Manmohan Singh government.

The other is an initiative for rooting out corruption from the Judiciary via the proposed National Judicial Council, which has been "under examination" of the chief justice for months.

However, some landmark initiatives need special mention. Two years ago, again following the Supreme Court's intervention, the government made the CVC the primary office for receiving complaints of whistle-blowers and passed the "Public Interest Disclosures and Protection of Informers" resolution.

Last year, the government brought in the "Right to Information" bill, which is increasingly being used to expose wrongdoing and corruption.

"Ensuring transparency and exposing corruption was one of the objectives of the government while bringing in the Right to Information Act," said Wajahad Habibullah, the country's first chief information commissioner. "I hope the act will be increasingly used for this."

For an alternative perspective, read the critical peer review commentary on this notebook, part of the 2006 Global Integrity Report (www.globalintegrity.org).

Indonesia:
Guns, Girls and HIV
By Andreas Harsono

Clad in a sarong and cotton shirt, Chief Sergeant Ukas seemes like an ordinary shopkeeper. He runs a family store next to his house on the outskirts of Merauke, a town in Indonesia's troubled Papua province. "I'm a retiree now," he says with a smile. In fact, Ukas retired from not one profession but two: the Army and the prostitution racket.

In 1996, when Ukas was the treasurer of the Merauke Military Command, he established the Nikita bar in downtown Merauke. Most town residents knew the Nikita made its money from the sex trade. "We usually bring in girls from Java or Makassar," Ukas said. "We contract them for three or four months. We also regularly check their health," he added.

Ukas is one of thousands of Indonesian military officers who profit from shadowy side jobs. Although they know it is illegal, the practice is so pervasive it's almost taken for granted. Even former President Suharto, the Army general who ruled Indonesia with an iron fist, was once demoted for smuggling. "Our salaries are not enough; we have to find extra income," Ukas argued.

Soldiers find ample opportunity in Indonesia, composed of thousands of islands stretching some 3,200 miles from east to west. Its 210 million people speak more than 500 different languages. Nearly 90 percent of its population is Muslim, concentrated on the islands of Java and Sumatra, though eastern provinces like Papua have a Christian majority.

Ethnic violence and separatist movements riddle Indonesia's modern history. Now many question whether Indonesia can survive as a nation-state given that its people's only common history is their Dutch colonial past. Suharto managed to keep the country together by brutal means after he rose to power in 1965, but after he left power in May 1998, the institutions he built began to crumble.

A common thread running through the chaos of Indonesian history is corruption within the Indonesian military (TNI—*Tentara Nasional Indonesia*). The New York-based group Human Rights Watch published a 126-page report in June 2006 titled "Too High a Price: The Human Rights Cost of the Indonesian Military's Economic Activities." The report described how the TNI raises money outside the government budget through a sprawling network of legal and illegal businesses.

An example is the large cache of military equipment found in the Jakarta houses of a dead Army general in June 2006 that included 145 weapons, 28,985 bullets, eight grenades, and 28 pairs of binoculars. Though the materiel was clearly moving through the black market, the TNI claimed

INDONESIA

The Global Integrity Index:
How effective are Indonesia's anti-corruption safeguards?

OVERALL RATING
Weak (68)

CATEGORY RATINGS

1) Civil Society, Public Information & Media — Very Weak (59)

2) Elections — Weak (69)

3) Government Accountability — Weak (62)

4) Administration & Civil Service — Moderate (72)

5) Oversight & Regulation — Moderate (70)

6) Anti-Corruption & Rule of Law — Moderate (74)

(Scores range from 0 to 100)

The Global Integrity Index, through the Integrity Indicators, assesses the existence and effectiveness of national anti-corruption mechanisms. It does not measure corruption itself (which is nearly impossible). Instead, the Index analyzes the opposite of corruption: the institutions and practices that promote more accountable government and prevent, deter or punish corruption.

The Index is based on nearly 300 Integrity Indicators, discrete scores assigned by local experts using a consistent methodology and scoring criteria for each country. These results are then blindly peer reviewed at the local and international level to ensure consistency and accuracy.

All of the more than 11,000 Integrity Indicator scores that comprise the 2006 Index are published—along with extensive commentary, references and critical peer review comments and perspectives—in the annual Global Integrity Report.

For full results and downloadable datasets, see the Global Integrity website (www.globalintegrity.org).

the general collected weapons as a "hobby."

The principal driver of military corruption is the fact that the military's budget is only partially covered by the government. Cornell University's Indonesia Journal estimated the government's contribution to be as low as 30 percent of the total. The TNI must raise the rest of the funds from three principal sources: *yayasan*, a complex system of non-governmental foundations; provision of services such as security and transportation for civilian clients including U.S. mining giant Freeport McMoran; and illegal businesses, such as protection rackets for prostitution and gambling businesses.

The lowest level of Army personnel, such as Sergeant Ukas, conduct the latter type of businesses, while private security services are largely managed by the *Kodam* (provincial-level Army command) and *Korem* (a subcommand). Only the *yayasan* are under direct control of the Army Central Command in Jakarta. The Asian economic crisis damaged the *yayasan*, exposing their endemic corruption and poor management. Army headquarters, however, found them difficult to investigate, as dozens of generals were involved. In 2001, Army headquarters finally understood that the *yayasan* bankruptcies posed a fundamental threat to the military institution and employed Ernst & Young to audit its biggest foundation, Yayasan Kartika Eka Paksi. The result was shocking: Only two of the 38 *yayasan* generated profits.

The Indonesian Parliament passed a law in 2004 requiring the TNI hand over all of its businesses to the government. The law mandates four ministries, including the defense and finance ministries, to audit some 1,500 military enterprises

INDONESIA

before turning them over by 2009. The TNI played hide-and-seek, however: A government team assigned to audit the firms estimated their total worth at only 1 trillion rupiah (US$100 million), far less than the value widely believed.

Their revelations took most legislators by surprise. "During the regime of former president Suharto, a number of generals held concessions for mining, forestry and other lucrative sectors inherited by TNI businesses, so the assets cannot be worth only 1 trillion rupiah," said lawmaker Permadi Satrio Wiwoho of the Indonesian Democratic Party of Struggle.

House member Soeripto of the Prosperous Justice Party expressed similar shock. "As someone who knows a little bit about forestry, I learned that one way or another, military members managed to get shares in all 550 logging concessions. How can there be only two concession-holders with connections to the military?" he said.

Ukas and his generals in Jakarta only echoed what founding president Sukarno repeatedly said about the Indonesian military: "It's a state within a state." Defense Minister Juwono Sudarsono is not surprised to hear stories like that of Ukas. "Bad cops and soldiers who are involved in protection rackets happen in Jakarta. You could also easily find them in Chicago or New York," he said.

But this kind of corruption does not only hurt the state. One of Ukas' girls was 25-year-old Anita Ayu Sulandari, who worked at the Nikita for three years until she decided to "freelance" in the hinterlands of Kaname Island. "I was considered old," she said. "In Kaname, I did business, looking for the *gaharu* in the villages." The *gaharu* tree produces a hard, black resin that the Asmat people burn to connect with their ancestors and cast spells. Outsiders value *gaharu* as the source of expensive incense for the Asian and Middle Eastern market. Ayu traded *gaharu* for sex, selling the *gaharu* to middlemen in Kaname. "If [the *gaharu*] is of low quality, one kilogram buys a short time," she said. "If the quality is excellent, it could be one full night."

In October 2002, Ayu fell seriously ill and returned to Merauke. Doctors told her that she had contracted HIV. Devastated, she decided to stay in a Catholic-run HIV treatment house. Last year, Ayu decided to leave the HIV medical treatment facility and worked again on the street. "I can't stand to live there. The [pocket] money was not enough. It's also hard to see my roommates die one by one," she said. I asked her if her consumers used condoms. "They said it is not natural," she answered.

An estimated 90,000 to 130,000 Indonesians are HIV positive, 30 percent of them in Papua, though the island contains only one percent of Indonesia's population. Papuan nationalists liken the spread of the disease to Indonesia's harsh military occupation. Corruption's role in both closes a deadly circle.

For an alternative perspective, read the critical peer review commentary on this notebook, part of the 2006 Global Integrity Report (www.globalintegrity.org).

INDONESIA

Israel:
Democracy in Decay

By Yossi Melman

In June 2006, three months after losing the Israeli
national election, Likud party leader Benjamin Netanyahu
said in an interview that Israeli business leaders tried to
bribe him when he served as Minister of the Treasury in the
previous government.

Reporters who knew the media-obsessed Netanyahu
assumed he was seeking to grab headlines and place himself once again at the center of Israeli social and economic
discourse. Nevertheless, such a statement would have led to
a public outcry and demand for police investigation in any
Western democratic country.

Though Israel considers itself part of the Western
democratic world, the news was received with widespread
indifference. Many Israelis share the feeling that in their
country "anything goes," even an attempt to bribe cabinet
ministers, and no human failure or wrongdoing surprise
them any longer.

These feelings long ago transformed into a notion that in terms of corruption—whether personal greed, political patronage or abuse of power—Israel is a third world country.

Some context: The last five prime ministers all came under police investigation, either while in office or after they left. Shimon Peres, Ehud Barak and Ariel Sharon were investigated for receiving illegal donations to their election campaigns; Benjamin Netanyahu for accepting expensive gifts and abusing state property. Sharon's investigation was particularly serious because of suspicions—never proven—indicating he had received kickbacks from Austrian casino kingpin Martin Schlaf.

The current premier Ehud Olmert is under two separate investigations for receiving bribes in dubious real estate deals (selling his posh Jerusalem flat to American billionaire Danny Abraham), and giving government jobs to cronies. He was cleared in a third investigation for receiving presents (for his prized pen collection). Justice Minister Haim Ramon had to resign in late 2006 to stand charges of sexual harassment of a young secretary. The Minister of Treasury, Avrahamm Hirschson is under another police investigation for stealing millions of Israeli new sheqalim (more than one million US dollars) fron non-profit organizations which he founded, including one dedicated to keeping the memory of the Holocaust. A Tel Aviv district court found him guilty and sentenced him to 120 hours of community work. President of the State, Moshe Katsav has been charged with rape, sexual harassment and abuse of his power. Yet he refused to resign and was forced by the Parliament to leave office temporarily.

Further investigations are underway on similar charges

ISRAEL

The Global Integrity Index:
How effective are Israel's anti-corruption safeguards?

OVERALL RATING

Strong (83)

CATEGORY RATINGS

1) Civil Society, Public Information & Media — Very Strong (92)

2) Elections — Very Strong (97)

3) Government Accountability — Weak (61)

4) Administration & Civil Service — Weak (68)

5) Oversight & Regulation — Very Strong (95)

6) Anti-Corruption & Rule of Law — Strong (87)

(Scores range from 0 to 100)

The Global Integrity Index, through the Integrity Indicators, assesses the existence and effectiveness of national anti-corruption mechanisms. It does not measure corruption itself (which is nearly impossible). Instead, the Index analyzes the opposite of corruption: the institutions and practices that promote more accountable government and prevent, deter or punish corruption.

The Index is based on nearly 300 Integrity Indicators, discrete scores assigned by local experts using a consistent methodology and scoring criteria for each country. These results are then blindly peer reviewed at the local and international level to ensure consistency and accuracy.

All of the more than 11,000 Integrity Indicator scores that comprise the 2006 Index are published—along with extensive commentary, references and critical peer review comments and perspectives—in the annual Global Integrity Report.

For full results and downloadable datasets, see the Global Integrity website (www.globalintegrity.org).

against three former cabinet ministers, at least 10 mayors and two dozen senior government officials. Additionally, five members of parliament (out of 120), including Omri Sharon, son of the former premier, have been indicted on various charges ranging from frauds to kickbacks, from falsifying university degrees to cheating on parliamentary votes.

The widespread corruption at the top is expressed as what is termed in Israel as the "tumorous" connections between capital and government (the words rhyme in Hebrew). Israeli business executives' access to and intimate relations with government officials give them inside information about future land deals, privatization, tax favors and other financial benefits.

As a result, a revolving-door tradition has been established. Take for example the case of Nir Gilad. Gilad was a young graduate from a local university who joined the Ministry of the Treasury twenty years ago and eventually reached the rank of deputy director general. He led a massive privatization process during his term which included the sale of Israel's national refineries to the Ofer brothers, one of the country's five richest families. The state lost nearly US$120 million on the sale because the tender was sloppily drafted. What did Gilad receive for his shoddy work? A job as deputy director general of the Ofer brothers' empire. Recently he was selected to lead the company.

Naturally, these worrisome trends are not confined to the power elite. Like malignant cells, they have spread to all walks of society in a system known as *macherim*, a Yiddish word originating in the Jewish Diaspora.

Macherim signifys everything Israel as a modern state

ISRAEL

wishes to negate. The word means "fixers," or middlemen who build a network of contacts with low-level government officials. Because of corruption, bureaucracy, lack of awareness and negligence, citizens struggle to get what they are entitled by law. Obtaining a driver's license, construction permit, hearing with the tax authorities or court appeal increasingly requires the fixer's intervention.

The results is that Israeli society has changed beyond recognition. Israel was once a role model, one of the most advanced and sophisticated social democracies. It was proud of its modern welfare system and tried to maintain as equal and just a society as possible.

The concept of *kibbutz*—a rural community guided by the principle that each receives according to his needs and gives back to society according to his abilities—was the jewel in Israel's crown. Today, the idea of the *kibbutz* is dying.

Israel now worships the golden calf of the free market: privatization and sink-or-swim competition, what British Prime Minster Edward Heath once called the "ugly face of capitalism." The country's economy is under the influence of a handful of families who, like robber barons, rob public assets, utilities and national resources, all with the help of corrupt officials and ministers.

To understand how few hands hold the country's wealth, one has to read the Israeli business daily The Marker. The paper estimates the accumulated wealth of the 500 richest people in the country at around 283 billion new sheqalim (US$65 billion). By contrast, Israel's GDP is 567 billion new sheqalim (US$130 billion), while its 2006 national budget is only 262 billion new sheqalim (US$60 billion).

Israel is now in the top ten nations with the widest so-cio-economic gap. Pensions have been reduced. Social security benefits have been cut.

In 2005, Israel produced more millionaires per capita than any other country. But it also pushed more people under the poverty line than any other western nation in the last decade.

Israel's Social Security Institute defines the poverty line as an income of 1,744 new sheqalim (US$400) per month per individual and less than 4,361 new sheqalim (US$1000) per family of four. One and half million people, or 20 percent of the population, live under the poverty line. Thirty-four percent of Israeli children live in poverty.

Fewer and fewer financial resources are allocated to public education, health, transportation and infrastructure. More and more go to the wealthy through tax cuts and other benefits aimed to protect capital gains. But perhaps the most worrisome aspect of the reduced public funds is its impact on law and order.

ISRAEL

Israeli police, already overstretched by Palestinian terrorism, lack the budget to fight crime. Police officers are underpaid and understaffed. They drive old cars or travel by bus to crime scenes. The notion of a friendly neighborhood police officer is unheard of; police officers are barely seen in the streets except after terrorist attacks. More and more police officers are under investigation for using excessive force against innocent citizens who come across their path.

No one answers the police emergency number. Thefts, car accidents and burglaries are no longer considered investigation-worthy. The very notion of law and order is being privatized;

security companies now provide basic services like street patrols and investigations to wealthy communities and corporations.

Major investigations and corruption cases are frozen by a lack of resources or a lack of will. Rather than investigate a real estate case worth 305 million new sheqalim (US$70 million) involving well-connected lawyers and politicians, the police prefer to focus on petty crimes, like small-scale social security fraud.

The few courageous police officers willing to work against the current find themselves under constant attack from politicians and wealthy billionaires, such as the Russian-French-Israeli fugitive Arcadi Gaydamak .

And when they seek support from one of the rare enclaves within the Ministry of Justice that is supposed to fight corruption, they are met by Minister of Justice Haim Ramon, known for his friendly ties to rich and powerful families. A few years ago, as a member of parliament, Ramon attended a wedding by an arms dealer in Monte Carlo. When asked by the House's ethics committee to pay back the expenses—private jet, luxurious hotel—he refused. In the summer of 2006, he came under investigation for sexual abuse of one of his secretaries. So much for justice.

Israel is still a vital democracy, but it is a democracy in decay. The champions of law, order and justice—the fighters of corruption—struggle upstream. In Israel, integrity is losing ground.

For an alternative perspective, read the critical peer review commentary on this notebook, part of the 2006 Global Integrity Report (www.globalintegrity.org).

Kenya:
Geography Lessons
By Mutegi Njau

During this year's World Cup soccer matches, Kenyans
—like many other Africans—learned for the first time the
names of countries new to the tournament, such as Croatia,
Serbia and Montenegro, and Trinidad and Tobago. Around
the same time, they learned of a country named Armenia for
a totally different reason: corruption.

Two alleged brothers from Armenia came to Kenya in
mid-2006 purporting to be investors. However, the "Atur
brothers" were in fact looting the government of security
equipment and documents, such as airport security passes,
police identity cards and Kenyan passports. A police raid on
their home recovered commando police uniforms, a cache
of arms from the presidential guard and stolen vehicles.
Knowledgeable sources say their activities could only have
been facilitated through high-level connections.

News of the scandal hit media headlines in March after
a police raid on Kenya's oldest newspaper, The Standard,

and its sister company Kenya Television Network. The raid was condemned locally and internationally as an affront to press freedom, but Internal Security Minister John Michuki defended the raid as necessary "in the interest of state security." President Mwai Kibaki was eventually compelled to establish a commission of inquiry on the matter.

The saga revealed the obstacles the country faces in effectively fighting its war on corruption. It is an uphill battle.

The struggle appeared to gain momentum in early 2006 following the disclosures by former Ethics and Governance Minister John Githongo on the Anglo Leasing affair, in which a fictitious company was given hundreds of millions of dollars in contracts. Three key cabinet ministers were forced to resign, ostensibly paving the way for investigations into the Anglo Leasing scandal, as well as another involving the Goldenberg International export company. No charges have thus far been filed against any of the ministers, and prosecution appears to be a distant possibility due to a lack of tangible evidence.

The higher echelons of government are not the only areas susceptible to corruption. Graft also weakened stringent traffic regulations, which lowered road accidents by 40 percent between 2004 and 2005. A study found that public transport vehicles involved in accidents carried loads weighing more than their legal capacity, had defective safety belts or did not have effective speed governors. One victim of such a smash-up was retired President Daniel arap Moi, who sustained serious injuries in an accident in July 2006.

The traffic police who are stationed on highways and

weighbridges are good examples of petty corruption in Kenya. Police constable Robert Mwangi, barely two years into service as a traffic officer, said his boss in Muranga demands a minimum of 2,000 shillings (US$30) every evening. "Even if I am given as little as 50 shillings (US$0.68) by a motorist I take it," he said bitterly.

Last February, authorities discovered that a constable stationed at Mariakani weighbridge in Mombasa had stashed 100,000 shillings (US$1,380) in his bed. Two colleagues manning a weighbridge at Gilgil, 600 kilometers inland from Mombasa, were later caught with 1.5 million shillings (US$20,500) in local and foreign currencies by the Kenya Anti-Corruption Commission. The Mariakani weighbridge handles an average of 2,000 vehicles daily, many of which pay upwards of 3,000 shillings (US$50) to pass through or as a protection fee. That adds up to more than 13.8 million shillings (US$190,000) a day! Consequently, excessive loads ruin many Kenyan highways.

The tourism industry also suffers from massive corruption. Game reserves around the country continue to shrink as a result of so-called private developers "grabbing" public land. Revenue from game reserve tourism, which should trickle down to rural communities, actually ends up in the bank accounts of corrupt politicians, tourism officers and administrators.

An April 2006 inter-ministerial task force report on national game reserve management by various county councils revealed monumental corruption in the Narok County Council, home of the fabled Masai Mara. The report said

KENYA

The Global Integrity Index:

How effective are Kenya's anti-corruption safeguards?

OVERALL RATING

Moderate (71)

CATEGORY RATINGS

1) Civil Society, Public Information & Media — Weak (68)

2) Elections — Weak (64)

3) Government Accountability — Very Weak (56)

4) Administration & Civil Service — Moderate (70)

5) Oversight & Regulation — Strong (89)

6) Anti-Corruption & Rule of Law — Moderate (79)

(Scores range from 0 to 100)

The Global Integrity Index, through the Integrity Indicators, assesses the existence and effectiveness of national anti-corruption mechanisms. It does not measure corruption itself (which is nearly impossible). Instead, the Index analyzes the opposite of corruption: the institutions and practices that promote more accountable government and prevent, deter or punish corruption.

The Index is based on nearly 300 Integrity Indicators, discrete scores assigned by local experts using a consistent methodology and scoring criteria for each country. These results are then blindly peer reviewed at the local and international level to ensure consistency and accuracy.

All of the more than 11,000 Integrity Indicator scores that comprise the 2006 Index are published—along with extensive commentary, references and critical peer review comments and perspectives—in the annual Global Integrity Report.

For full results and downloadable datasets, see the Global Integrity website (www.globalintegrity.org).

4,000 acres were illegally shaved from Kenya's world-fa-
mous wildlife sanctuary, Masai Mara Game Reserve, and
another 4,000 acres from Masai Mau Forest. The land was
allocated to a former council treasurer, who is the son of
the late Masai paramount chief and brother of an assistant
minister in the ruling Narc government. The family is the
largest landowner in Narok District. When the allocation was cancelled in October 2000, the assistant minister
enlisted the law firm of current director of public prosecutions, Keraiko Tobiko, in his brother's defense.

Corruption also leads to markets near game park entrances, such as the Sekenani, Ololaimutia and Mararianda
markets at Masai Mara. Besides being eyesores, these markets pose a security risk to visitors. Still, permission to erect
the structures can be obtained through unofficial fees ranging from 75,000 to 750,000 shillings (US$1,000-10,000)
depending on size and location, according to Maasai Mara
Senior Game Warden Michael ole Koikai. A 2005 audit of
Masai Mara Game Reserve tourism fees revealed that millions of shillings were misappropriated or unaccounted for.
Another report by the Council's internal auditor unearthed
a 22,860,000 shilling (US$300,0000) embezzlement scam.
Such money would go a long way in providing health and
educational facilities, as well as livestock husbandry services, to the marginalized Masai community in Narok.

The Masai Mara Game Reserve is not an isolated case:
Tourism Minister Morris Dzoro exposed a scandal in 2006,
in which staff looted the ministry in excess of 200 million
shillings (US$2.8 million) every year. Nearly 75 ministry

KENYA

staffers and tour drivers were involved in the racket.

But delivering justice in Kenya remains an elusive and expensive exercise in terms of both time and money. The backlog of cases stretches back for more than a decade, while thousands of innocent Kenyans languish in over-crowded prisons. The situation has forced individuals to seek the direct intervention of officials such as Chief Justice Evans Gicheru. One distraught Kenyan, Bahadur Lalji Nurani, wrote to Gicheru in May 2006 demanding hearings on numerous cases that have kept Nurani in judicial limbo for more than a decade. Most rulings were "a rich cocktail of intrigue and judicial improprieties...thanks to the power of money and capricious minds," Nurani wrote. Nurani also gathered the courage to sue the formerly untouchable politician Nicholas Biwott for failing to pay for the family's two farms in Eldoret after 22 years. Progress on the case dragged so slowly that after a year of silence, he also sought intervention from Paul Muite, his lawyer and a member of Parliament.

For an alternative perspective, read the critical peer review commentary on this notebook, part of the 2006 Global Integrity Report (www.globalintegrity.org).

Kyrgyz Republic:
Revolution for Sale

By Yulia Savchenko

Corruption in Kyrgyzstan has long inhabited every office
in the Kyrgyz White House, especially its seventh floor, where
president and other top-ranking officials "serve" the people.
In 2005, amid allegations of unprecedented corruption, President Askar Akaev was deposed in a popular uprising. The
country's new leadership proudly announced that they would
put an end to corruption in the Kyrgyz Republic.

Recently we Kyrgyz celebrated the first anniversary
of this promising announcement, begging the question of
whether anyone has enjoyed any results thus far. Some probably have, but I have never met these optimists.

The top-down initiative of fighting corruption has never
been marked by any visible progress on the ground. Prime
Minister Felix Kulov seemed to be the only official who
sincerely believed in the idea of rooting out corruption. In the
early days of his office, Kulov announced that neither he nor
his family members would ever be involved in any entrepre-

neurial activities in the Kyrgyz Republic.

Despite the fierce fight with corruption in the high echelons of power in the aftermath of the "Tulip Revolution,"
the role model set by the prime minister has never become an
overly appealing one on any floor of the White House. The latest civil protests in June 2006 in Bishkek called on the power-
holders to put an end to the rampant corruption. The slogans
of protesters read "President—stop serving your pockets!" and
"No to the MAXIMization of economy" (referring to Maxim,
the eldest son of president Kurmanbek Bakiev). Lots of people
already have a strong feeling of déjà vu; the Politburo kids
always liked doing business in the Kyrgyz Republic.

However, it's not that other people in the country are
standing still, lacking imagination. We tend to excel when it
comes to making money illegally. One fascinating phenomenon surfaced during the days of "people's" revolution and
kept flourishing afterwards: buying civic activism.

No, you didn't misread anything. Rumor has it that
the rate to inspire people for expressing will, opinion and
sometimes outrage varies nowadays from 100 to 1000 soms
(US$3 to US$25).

One of the first experiments of this practice was an
unquestionable success. A crowd of "protesters" on June 17,
2005, stormed the White House for the second time since
the March revolution, demanding that their "candidate,"
well known Kazakh businessman Urmatbek Baryktabasov,
be registered as a member of parliament. The protests of
this "frustrated electorate" were well organized. I saw buses
packed with protesters come to downtown Bishkek from local

districts. Upon leaving the buses, the crowd was instructed
where to move and what to shout. Demonstrators got free
transportation, free food and beverages, plus minor payments
for the expression of their "free will." Once the event was
over, participants rushed to cars inconspicuously arranged
at the perimeter of the main square in downtown Bishkek to
collect their earnings.

The process was videotaped, but no one was prosecuted.
It was one of the first cases of the reverse corruption—politicians offering money to ordinary citizens. Exciting!

In their daily affairs, Kyrgyz citizens are used to bribing officials for documents or services they need. In a country where average monthly salaries are only 4,000 soms
(US$100) at best, a fortune often is charged for processing
paperwork when it needs to be done reasonably quickly or, in
some cases, to be done at all.

A recent example is the campaign to issue new national
passports in the Kyrgyz Republic. Here I can be very personal
since in June 2005 my passport expired. I urgently needed
to get a new document simply to be able to function as a
citizen (there is a saying here that you are a bug if you don't
have your paper) and to be able to apply for a visa to the
United States. The timing in my case was most unfortunate:
The nationwide campaign on exchanging national passports,
launched under the previous government, was deadlocked
due to corruption questions. New passport forms were stuck
somewhere in Moldova and so presumably no passports were
being issued in the Kyrgyz Republic.

After a number of desperate calls to a number of state

KYRGYZ REPUBLIC

The Global Integrity Index:
How effective are the Kyrgyz Republic's anti-corruption safeguards?

OVERALL RATING
Weak (64)

CATEGORY RATINGS

1) Civil Society, Public Information & Media — Weak (67)

2) Elections — Weak (60)

3) Government Accountability — Weak (64)

4) Administration & Civil Service — Very Weak (56)

5) Oversight & Regulation — Moderate (78)

6) Anti-Corruption & Rule of Law — Very Weak (57)

(Scores range from 0 to 100)

The Global Integrity Index, through the Integrity Indicators, assesses the existence and effectiveness of national anti-corruption mechanisms. It does not measure corruption itself (which is nearly impossible). Instead, the Index analyzes the opposite of corruption: the institutions and practices that promote more accountable government and prevent, deter or punish corruption.

The Index is based on nearly 300 Integrity Indicators, discrete scores assigned by local experts using a consistent methodology and scoring criteria for each country. These results are then blindly peer reviewed at the local and international level to ensure consistency and accuracy.

All of the more than 11,000 Integrity Indicator scores that comprise the 2006 Index are published—along with extensive commentary, references and critical peer review comments and perspectives—in the annual Global Integrity Report.

For full results and downloadable datasets, see the Global Integrity website (www.globalintegrity.org).

agencies, I found out that a dozen or so new passport forms were "reserved for special cases." For my case to qualify as "special," I was supposed to pay as much as $600—unofficially, of course. That same fixed rate popped up in my discussions with other desperate passport-seekers. Apparently many people were charged the same amount for having their passports done urgently, in spite of the promises of the newly elected government to put an end to corruption. The saga unfolded for almost a year until the head of the Department of Passport and Visa Regimes was finally sent to jail for abusing power. He was released after a couple of months.

This is a common scenario: Law enforcement agencies catch officials taking bribes, the officials are imprisoned, then other agencies see that they are released. According to a Ministry of Internal Affairs representative, 150 officials who took bribes were detained during the first six months of 2006, twice as many as during the same period of the previous year. The main question here is how many charges are dropped on their way to Kyrgyz courts?

On the surface, authorities in the Kyrgyz Republic pursue a "persistent" policy of rooting out corruption. Indeed, if we glance back at all anti-corruption efforts of the power holders in the republic, we find an impressive scale and a variety of actions. In 1999 President Akaev pioneered the process with the Law Against Corruption. In 2003 the Council for Good Governance was established under the patronage of the prime minister. Immediately after the revolution, President Bakiev said that the priority of the new government would be fighting corruption in all spheres. A special state body named

KYRGYZ REPUBLIC

National Agency of the Kyrgyz Republic for Prevention of Corruption was established. A year after he uttered his famous words we at least can say that the good will was there. In terms of the political impetus given it's not bad at all—for starters. In terms of the real-life practices, though, there have been no concrete consequences or changes for those who fall victim to the widespread tradition of paying their way through everyday life.

The World Bank recently conducted a study on the dynamics of corruption in 26 post-Soviet countries. The study demonstrates that only Kyrgyzstan and Russia, among those listed, failed in their anti-corruption efforts.

For a bystander, life in Kyrgyzstan appears to be a chain of never-ending financial acts of gratitude for everyday civil services. We need to be grateful to doctors (if we want to stay alive after their interventions), to the educators of our kids, to judges and policemen. And of course to a variety of bureaucrats for the work they do, which is, by the way, already rewarded by taxpayers' gratitude.

According to a survey conducted by the Center for the Study of Public Opinion in Kyrgyzstan, people "normally" show their gratitude by offering money to customs control system (93 percent of respondents), police (90 percent) and the courts and judiciary (66 percent). Among the most corrupt organization were customs, tax inspection (92 percent), militia and departments of internal affairs (90 percent) and the state auto inspection (89 percent). Thus it's indeed safe to conclude that the majority of the population is pessimistic about the Kyrgyz government's ambition to bring corruption to its knees.

The truth is the president himself is far less enthusiastic about fighting the corruption now than he was a year ago. Recently, in a voice full of hesitation, Bakiev said during one of his televised addresses: "We should deal with corruption. We should at least try to decrease it ... somehow."

For an alternative perspective, read the critical peer review commentary on this notebook, part of the 2006 Global Integrity Report (www.globalintegrity.org).

KYRGYZ REPUBLIC

Lebanon:
Citizen or Shareholder?

By Maha Al-Azar

When the fifteen-year Lebanese civil war ended and the reconstruction process was set into motion, then-Prime Minister Rafik Hariri came up with a revolutionary idea. In 1994 he created a private company called Solidere, an acronym for *Société Libanaise de Développement et Réconstruction* (Lebanese Company for the Development and Reconstruction). All Lebanese, including government officials, could be shareholders.

In many ways, Solidere could be considered a microcosm of corruption in the Lebanese system, representing many of the problems existing throughout the country.

To begin with, it operates in a sort of gray area, being a private company subject to commercial laws while performing a very public function. It also is a prime example of conflict of interest—its primary shareholder also is the head of the executive branch of the country, putting him in a position to award government contracts to his own company.

Finally, all Lebanese are potential shareholders (part of the company's selling point), giving them a motive to maintain the system of corruption.

"Every Lebanese has become a shareholder in the corruption system," says Jawad Adra, who heads Information International, a private company that regularly conducts polls and studies on the public's perception of various issues, including corruption.

Professor George Yacoub, in his unpublished study "Lebanon Security Dilemma: A Strategic Reading into Lebanon's Political History," argues that "the great majority of Lebanese, regardless of religion, social status, location, political affiliations or wealth are unwilling to change the present system, not because they are blind to its hazards, but because they have developed a stake in maintaining it."

Indeed, corruption has become internalized and systemized to the point that small bribes are often considered "tips" and grand scale personal benefit from holding public office is, in the Lebanese psyche, often considered "cleverness."

It is this general acquiescence to the corrupt status quo, combined with the pursuit of personal over public interest that keeps corrupt people from being scandalized or the news media from actually investigating alleged cases of corruption. In fact, all major TV stations but one (NewTV), are at least partially owned by a government official. This privately owned TV station, NewTV, only recently started broadcasting a program that addresses cases of corruption, a few months before the Syrian troop withdrawal from Lebanon in April 2005. This program, called *Fassad* (Corruption), has

LEBANON

The Global Integrity Index:
How effective are Lebanon's anti-corruption safeguards?

OVERALL RATING

Very Weak (51)

CATEGORY RATINGS

1) Civil Society, Public Information & Media — Weak (63)

2) Elections — Very Weak (38)

3) Government Accountability — Very Weak (59)

4) Administration & Civil Service — Very Weak (42)

5) Oversight & Regulation — Very Weak (56)

6) Anti-Corruption & Rule of Law — Very Weak (48)

(Scores range from 0 to 100)

The Global Integrity Index, through the Integrity Indicators, assesses the existence and effectiveness of national anti-corruption mechanisms. It does not measure corruption itself (which is nearly impossible). Instead, the Index analyzes the opposite of corruption: the institutions and practices that promote more accountable government and prevent, deter or punish corruption.

The Index is based on nearly 300 Integrity Indicators, discrete scores assigned by local experts using a consistent methodology and scoring criteria for each country. These results are then blindly peer reviewed at the local and international level to ensure consistency and accuracy.

All of the more than 11,000 Integrity Indicator scores that comprise the 2006 Index are published—along with extensive commentary, references and critical peer review comments and perspectives—in the annual Global Integrity Report.

For full results and downloadable datasets, see the Global Integrity website (www.globalintegrity.org).

been touted by many as a flagship for raising awareness about corruption. As a result, its host, Ghada Eid, often receives threats to her life because of the controversial topics she raises in her program.

Similarly, in 2001, when a United Nations-commissioned report on corruption named Hariri allies involved in corruption, Hariri took it out on the National Integrity Steering Committee to Fight Corruption, blaming it for allowing the report to be publicized. As a result, the committee's work was frozen by Hariri and has not been reactivated since.

Many blame sectarianism and its resulting clientalism for the current state of corruption.

Each sect leader always favors people from his own sect for public appointments. For this reason, ministries headed by a minister of one sect are mostly staffed by personnel belonging to the same sect.

Member of Parliament Ghassan Mokheiber, a member of the opposition, said that the duty-free zone at the airport was allegedly leased out "for peanuts" to Prime Minister Fuad Siniora's close friend. Lately, news reports have accused the Sunni-led government of favoring Sunni appointments to security agencies.

In contrast, the cost of corruption on the Lebanese economy was estimated at about 1.5 trillion pounds (US$1 billion) annually in a 2000 study. This should not come as a surprise, since a 2001 U.N.-commissioned report mentioned that out of 9 trillion pounds (US$6 billion) in project expenditures, only 2.4 percent (US$143 million) was awarded by the state Administration of Tenders. The remainder did not

LEBANON

go to the most qualified applicants, but to those willing to pay the highest bribes.

But the problem remains one of lack of accountability, argues Adnan Iskandar, a public administration expert. Indeed, no matter how many reports come out regarding an alleged case of corruption, one rarely ever hears of anyone being penalized.

In 2002, documentary evidence implicating former agriculture minister Ali Abdullah in embezzlement and fraud did not lead to his prosecution. It was only after he was ousted from the Amal movement to which he belonged and his immunity stripped that his successor personally pursued legal action against him (in 2003), leading to his trial and prosecution.

One of the major corruption scandals that still makes headline news to this day is the 2003 Al-Madina Bank scandal, in which high-ranking Lebanese and Syrian officials were allegedly implicated in money-laundering, fraud and the misappropriation of funds amounting to losses of over 1.5 trillion pounds (US$1 billion) to depositors. To date, no clear convictions, barring brief arrests, have been made, fueling suspicions that powerful politicians had been involved.

After the war, both Hariri and former Prime Minister Salim Hoss, each during their terms in office, tried to carry out reforms and purge the administration from corrupt elements. Neither succeeded, and both were criticized for only punishing those from a different political group or those with no political backing. In many cases, those purged or scandalized returned to assume posts in the government.

Even government officials acknowledge that it is not

possible to penalize people.

"Very few people have been penalized for accepting bribes for several reasons," said Roger Melki, a senior advisor at the Ministry of Finance. "First, [the corrupt staff] protect each other. Secondly, the end user never reports bribes or complains, as he considers it's not worth his while...Even the few cases that were penalized did not act as deterrent to others, because political interference causes them to be released."

In cases when people actually seek justice, the government tries to paralyze oversight bodies, either directly or indirectly, by pressuring judges. During the 2005 parliamentary elections, 11 candidates contested the results of the election, alleging vote-buying by the winners. The response was that the government has halted the work of the Constitutional Council, the body that examines the validity of election results and constitutionality of laws, on the grounds that the terms of five of the 10-member council had expired. But it has also refused to appoint replacements, effectively freezing the body's work. As a result, 11 seats in parliament are currently contested, but the members of parliament filling these seats are passing laws and going about their business as usual.

In parallel, reports of judges being pressured to issue a certain verdict abound, despite lack of conclusive legal measures against a single judge.

Similarly, other oversight mechanisms are also dysfunctional because of the absence of laws that support transparency and accountability.

LEBANON

129

Member of Parliament Mokheiber argues that parliamentarians do not have the infrastructure and support
system needed to properly monitor the executive branch.
Presently, business hours at Parliament are from 8 a.m. to 2
p.m., after which all support staff exit the building, leaving
members of parliament to fend for themselves—should they
choose to work after hours. But such short working hours
do not permit members of parliament to successfully do
their work, especially since none of them have research as-
sistants or aides to help them in their oversight responsibili-
ties. Mokheiber says that bills for enhancing the efficiency
and building the capacity of Parliament are required, in addition to bills on access to information and public reporting
that would compel public servants and officials to disclose
how they are spending public money.

Although everyone, from public servants to businessmen to members of parliament, acknowledges that bribery
takes place in the administration, they also all agree that
any step toward computerization will likely curb such
practices by minimizing contact between citizens and public
servants. A number of transactions, such as the declarations
of the Value-Added-Tax, have been computerized over the
past five years, prompting many to be hopeful of the future.
Moreover, recruitment procedures have over the past year
been gradually standardized and tests are administered by
independent, government-appointed committees of experts,
something which Iskandar believes will improve the quality
of public servants that are hired.

While polling shows these measures did not improve

public perceptions of corruption, they leave some hope for the next generation to do better than this one, focusing on reform, in addition to reconstruction and development.

For an alternative perspective, read the critical peer review commentary on this notebook, part of the 2006 Global Integrity Report (www.globalintegrity.org).

LEBANON

Liberia:
The Leaking Government

By Cheechiay Jablasone

Liberia, with its population of nearly 3 million and civil service of 47,000, subsisted on a budget of 5.1 billion Liberian dollars (US$85) million from July 2005 to June 2006. Why? Because most of the government's revenue vanished into the pockets of its own employees.

An example: Most of this West African state's revenue comes from tariffs on imports, but securing this revenue is difficult due to leakage in a customs system which financial experts say lacks accountability mechanisms.

The country currently draws its revenue from four public corporations: the National Port Authority, Roberts International Airport, the Maritime Program and the Liberia Petroleum Refinery Company, which now only provides storage facilities for importers.

Due to "weak management and operational systems" at most of these corporations, and abuse of the "letter" payment system under the transitional government, Liberia's international partners—the United States, United Nations, European Union, African Union, Economic Community of West African States, International Monetary Fund and World Bank—expressed serious concerns about the country's economic governance.

These concerns resulted in the creation of the Governance and Economic Management Assistance Program (GEMAP), which aims to reorganize Liberia's financial system. GEMAP experts are currently working to improve budgeting, expenditure management and procurement practices, in addition to overseeing concession granting and reorganizing the tax system.

The program assigns a chief IMF administrator with executive authority to the Central Bank of Liberia. Controllers with co-signing authority are also assigned to each of the four public corporations as well as to the Forestry Development Authority, a large agency currently prevented from generating revenue by a forestry policy review.

A series of audits of state-owned enterprises by the European Union and an investigation by the Economic Community of West African States in the second quarter of 2005 brought some degree of sanity to the transitional government. However, the present administration sees GEMAP as a tool in curbing corruption and not an end to corruption in itself.

Corruption pervades the tax system. The minister of finance disclosed in June 2006 that charitable organizations were abusing their duty-free privilege by importing items into the country duty free and then commercializing them.

LIBERIA

The Global Integrity Index:
How effective are Liberia's anti-corruption safeguards?

OVERALL RATING

Very Weak (57)

CATEGORY RATINGS

1) Civil Society, Public Information & Media — Moderate (73)

2) Elections — Moderate (71)

3) Government Accountability — Very Weak (57)

4) Administration & Civil Service — Very Weak (33)

5) Oversight & Regulation — Very Weak (49)

6) Anti-Corruption & Rule of Law — Very Weak (56)

(Scores range from 0 to 100)

The Global Integrity Index, through the Integrity Indicators, assesses the existence and effectiveness of national anti-corruption mechanisms. It does not measure corruption itself (which is nearly impossible). Instead, the Index analyzes the opposite of corruption: the institutions and practices that promote more accountable government and prevent, deter or punish corruption.

The Index is based on nearly 300 Integrity Indicators, discrete scores assigned by local experts using a consistent methodology and scoring criteria for each country. These results are then blindly peer reviewed at the local and international level to ensure consistency and accuracy.

All of the more than 11,000 Integrity Indicator scores that comprise the 2006 Index are published—along with extensive commentary, references and critical peer review comments and perspectives—in the annual Global Integrity Report.

For full results and downloadable datasets, see the Global Integrity website (www.globalintegrity.org).

The duty-free exemption has since been suspended and is now under review.

But while the government vigorously pursues tax collection, sources at the customs commission say most appointed officials who previously resided in the United States refuse to pay a three-percent duty imposed on their personal effects. A junior official at the government procurement office who imported his personal effects refused to pay a duty amounting to just 21,148 dollars (US$351).

While the government's housecleaning effort marches on, some are finding new ways to sidestep it. As I joked over lunch with a procurement office employee from a local government ministry that the Governance and Economic Management Assistance Program had finally stymied corruption, he told me how GEMAP regulations are regularly bypassed by employees who swap budget line items such as gasoline and maintenance services. He said several of his bosses collect cash and gasoline supplies from vendors for their own purposes, knowing financial experts would have no way of tracking how exhaustible supplies are used.

A former colleague who now works in the accounts section at another government ministry also explained to me how "unscrupulous" people doing business with the government increase—sometimes even double—profit margins by swapping cheaper goods for budget items or discounting government services in exchange for cash they pocket.

Engaging in corruption under the present administration could be quite a risky venture. In May 2006, President Ellen Johnson-Sirleaf dismissed four junior officials from the health, commerce and transport ministries for "improprieties."

Two of the officials, one from the health ministry and another from the transport ministry, challenged their dismissals. Though the government has promised to turn the officials over for prosecution, they have yet to be tried.

The coming years should test the government's "zero tolerance" approach toward fighting corruption. In its first six months, Liberia's new House and Senate have yet to ratify the United Nations and African Union conventions on corruption.

While waiting for the Senate's ratification of these conventions, in spring 2006 the Governance Reform Commission initiated a national anti-corruption strategy policy session with government officials and civil society organizations, producing a national anti-corruption strategy policy paper.

The policy paper outlines several steps for combating corruption: ratifying the UN and AU conventions; introducing a code of conduct for public servants; encouraging participation across civil society; improving expenditure control in central and local governments as well as state corporations; and ensuring accountable and transparent financial management.

It also calls for the government to implement transparent procurement and contracting practices, develop an efficient and independent general auditing office, and strengthen the public accounts committee and other, related committees in the legislature that provide oversight and compliance.

The strategy paper also calls for "Reviewing existing laws and enacting anti-corruption legislation which will establish an independent anti-corruption institution."

The document already faces legal and statutory battles,

especially regarding its recommendation to establish an independent anti-corruption commission. As Liberia's justice minister has said, her office holds sole prosecutorial power in the government, meaning an independent prosecutor cannot be installed in absence of an amendment or repeal of the laws establishing the ministry.

In the face of the public debate the strategy paper will likely generate, if it goes before the legislators that leave for break on August 31, to return next January, the justice ministry will retain responsibility for prosecuting corruption charges.

Following a wave of public pressure, the government agreed to prosecute former officials linked to corrupt practices, claiming it was gathering evidence to pass on to the justice ministry. Gyude Bryant, head of the transitional government, was named along with several other government officials in a 2005 Economic Community of West African States report as likely to have engaged in misappropriations of public finances.

Regardless of GEMAP's short term gains, President Sirleaf has termed corruption in the country "systemic." This is no longer about control mechanisms; it's about a change of attitude.

Even in the face of rigid financial control mechanisms, Liberia's bloated civil service still needs improvement. At least 7,500 civil servants are "ghosts," according to the Civil Service Agency, meaning they only exist on government payrolls so corrupt officials can take their monthly salary.

With average monthly salaries at 850 dollars (US$15), the Liberian government loses about 12.8 million dollars

LIBERIA

(US$100,000) to government corruption each month. Soon, salaries for the lowest-paid civil servants are expected to climb to between 1,567 dollars (US$26) and 1,808 dollars (US$30). To prevent the creation of more ghosts due to these new salaries, the government will reduce its workforce of 47,000 to 35,000. About 5,000 employees are expected to be pensioned, while the rest are "ghosts," according to the CSA.

Petty corruption is also widespread in Liberia, especially in the form of bribery for processing documents like passports, drivers' licenses and birth certificates. The Center for Transparency and Accountability in Liberia says such forms of corruption are common due to the lack of "procedural information" at government agencies.

The government and its partners have thus far only been able to look at controlling expenditures and revenue collection: Nothing is being done so far to install such procedural guidelines at government agencies. This is the next step in Liberia's fight against corruption.

For an alternative perspective, read the critical peer review commentary on this notebook, part of the 2006 Global Integrity Report (www.globalintegrity.org).

Mexico:
Petty Victories

By Leonarda Reyes

On a busy street in the center of Mexico City, a woman talked with transit agents. The woman was outraged. You could see it and feel it. Suddenly, she jumped on the hood of a parked car, to the shock of the agents. The car was hers, which only made the scene more bizarre.

Who would you believe if the lady had filed a municipal complaint saying her car was damaged—the agents or the offended citizen? Luckily for the agents, the whole scene was taped by a video camera installed in the municipal tow truck. It showed her trying to prevent the car from being towed away after parking it illegally.

"There was a lot of tension with towing vehicles every day," said an official. "Then there were complaints that the traffic agents asked for money or that they damaged the vehicles. Video cameras helped solve that problem."

While some problems have simple solutions, other forms of corruption prove harder to stop. Thousands of illegal taxis are allowed to work on the streets of Mexico City as long as they carry a Black Panther sticker on the front window. It means the taxi is protected by an organization linked to the leftist party, PRD (*Partido de la Revolución Democrática*). Cab drivers have to pay a monthly fee to the organization. The code varies depending on what political party is in power in what state. There are a dozen of such informal organizations in Mexico City and many more all around the country.

"Here, I have the papers," says a taxi driver, showing me a blue folder while crossing through a green light. In the folder he has copies of what is supposed to be a legal case claiming the right to an honest job. He belongs to a small organization and pays a monthly fee of some 150 pesos (US$14). In addition, he is obligated to attend PRD political demonstrations when required.

Both sides benefit from the transaction. The PRD gets support, while the illegal taxi drivers don't pay as much for municipal permits as the legal drivers do. But in the overall scheme, the city loses millions of tax dollars that are left out of the public financial system.

In Mexico, a driver's license or a passport (the first a local procedure, the latter a federal one) can be obtained in just hours. You can pay only the official fees and avoid standing in long lines or sitting in crowded waiting rooms. Services like telephone lines or electricity are easy to get without a bribe.

But this improvement in Mexico's history of everyday corruption has been uneven. Secretaries in civil judges' offices might now refuse to take money to put your files ahead of other cases and speed up the legal process. But in another case, I saw a court employee demand more than 1,086 pesos (US$100) to produce some documents.

However, let's not miss the point about corruption. These small bribes and extortions show up in international polls and the local media. But they are petty corruption. It is visible day-to-day and affects millions of people, but this is by no means the most damaging form of corruption when you follow the money.

Paying 22 to 54 pesos (US$2 to US$3) to park illegally, bribing to get a public service installed or to sell goods on the street costs citizens an estimated in 18 billion pesos (US$1.7 billion) a year. However, overall corruption in Mexico is estimated to cost the country at least 35 times more, 651 billion pesos (US$60 billion) a year. This grand corruption requires access to much larger pots of money.

Alstom, a global power company headquartered in Paris, knew how to do business in Mexico. To win two contracts worth 62 million pesos (US$5.7 million) the company allegedly paid 7 million pesos (US$653,000) to Alfonso Caso and another top executive at Light and Power Center (LFC— *Luz y Fuerza Centro*), which provides electricity to Mexico City and four surrounding states. The Alstom office in Paris approved the bribe payment, according to executives under federal protection.

Former President Vicente Fox's government kept the investigation under seal until December 2005 when a press release was issued about a 325,470 pesos (US$30,000) fine imposed on Alstom, and a two-year ban on participating in public contract tenders. There was no word of criminal charges

MEXICO

The Global Integrity Index:
How effective are Mexico's
anti-corruption safeguards?

OVERALL RATING

Weak (65)

CATEGORY RATINGS

1) Civil Society, Public Information & Media — Moderate (72)

2) Elections — Moderate (76)

3) Government Accountability — Weak (61)

4) Administration & Civil Service — Very Weak (55)

5) Oversight & Regulation — Weak (69)

6) Anti-Corruption & Rule of Law — Very Weak (58)

(Scores range from 0 to 100)

The Global Integrity Index, through the Integrity Indicators, assesses the existence and effectiveness of national anti-corruption mechanisms. It does not measure corruption itself (which is nearly impossible). Instead, the Index analyzes the opposite of corruption: the institutions and practices that promote more accountable government and prevent, deter or punish corruption.

The Index is based on nearly 300 Integrity Indicators, discrete scores assigned by local experts using a consistent methodology and scoring criteria for each country. These results are then blindly peer reviewed at the local and international level to ensure consistency and accuracy.

All of the more than 11,000 Integrity Indicator scores that comprise the 2006 Index are published—along with extensive commentary, references and critical peer review comments and perspectives—in the annual Global Integrity Report.

For full results and downloadable datasets, see the Global Integrity website (www.globalintegrity.org).

and the name of the former director was not included.

Disclosures like this are sporadic. Polls can give evidence of the real extent of corruption. A study found that one in 10 companies admitted paying bribes to get contracts, concessions or favorable legal orders to influence changes in laws, policies and regulations. But this form of corruption usually does not get much attention from the news media.

In Los Pinos, the presidential residence in Mexico City, former President Fox sat in a meeting surrounded by secretaries and high-level officials. The meeting's purpose was to improve the state of government corruption. After hearing about a lack of progress, Fox asked why the perception of corruption was still so common in the country and how to solve the problem. Secretary Eduardo Romero—head of the anti-corruption effort—explained both.

Impunity is what most influences the perception of civil society, Romero said, giving two examples of cases that went unpunished during the Fox administration. "Such cases leave the impression in the public that the government tends to defend corrupt people," he said.

Romero added another key point: Fox's government emphasized prevention, not punishment. "There are weaknesses in the sanctioning regime. This is in addition to the weaknesses in the justice system," he said.

Of course, we can assume that no one in that meeting mentioned that Fox's own family has been tarnished by allegations of corruption. Accusations have been levied against the sons of his wife, Marta Sahagun. A special commission in the House of Representatives found that Sahagun's son

MEXICO

Manuel used his influence to earn millions of dollars. The evidence showed the first lady must have been aware of his enrichment, the commission said.

The first lady fired back, calling the legislator heading the House commission, Jesus Gonzalez Schmal a "liar" and a "coward." She maintains the accusations against her son have no grounds. High profile cases are rarely prosecuted and might take years to be heard in court. Meanwhile, the federal and state prosecutors are busy putting low-level criminals in jail.

"Our justice system focuses on punishing the poorest and the least dangerous criminals—those who cannot pay bribes. It is extremely unjust to punish minor crimes and minor robberies. We all lose because all the mafias—narcotics traffickers, car stealing mafias—get stronger," said Ana Laura Magaloni, a scholar with the Center for Economic Investigation and Education (*Centro de Investigación y Docencia Económicas*—CIDE).

Judges, often perceived as corrupt, might suffer from a different problem.

"We believe judges are weak instead of corrupt. They are not eager to confront the facts of what happens during detention and the prosecutors' investigations. In 96 percent of cases, judges issue a guilty decision. That means they are giving ground to the prosecutors," Magaloni said, citing a CIDE study that will be published soon.

Whether the cause is weakness or corruption, the impact on the lives of the people trapped in the justice system is the same. But for the powerful, the rules are different.

Marco Antonio Hernandez, a teenager driving with three friends, was killed by the driver of a black BMW in a traffic incident. The police arrived quickly and minutes after an alert was issued the police stopped a black BMW driven by Federico Ruiz Lomeli, 29, the son a prominent family in the state of Queretaro, in central Mexico, where this story played out. Lomeli, along with his friends in the car, were briefly questioned and released on the spot.

Lomeli was never charged with the murder nor confronted with a key witness who publicly identified the alleged killer after seeing Lomeli's photograph in a local paper. The National Human Rights Commission (CNDH —*Comisión Nacional de los Derechos Humanos*) found other wrong-doings in the case, but nothing changed. The killing is still unpunished.

In the end, seeing the long arm of the law for the many and impunity for the powerful, leads to no other conclusion than this: to stop petty street corruption, grand ruling class corruption or any corruption for that matter, the change has to start with the politicians at the top. All Mexicans agree on that. But today, Mexico's strategy on fighting corruption is starting at the bottom. It is working in the wrong direction as it has for decades.

For an alternative perspective, read the critical peer review commentary on this notebook, part of the 2006 Global Integrity Report (www.globalintegrity.org).

MEXICO

Republic of Montenegro:
The Power of Denial

By Zoran Radulovic

"Corruption is not a part of the tradition of the people in Montenegro." That's how Montenegrin government officials reacted to the U.S. State Department's 2005 human rights report, which said, "Corruption was a problem; the small, close-knit society discouraged reporting corruption and provided criminals access to law enforcement officers."

On July 31, 2006, the Montenegrin Parliament refused to adopt a new draft law, which was supported by the Council of Europe, on preventing conflicts of interest. In fact, parliamentarians from the ruling and opposition parties both rejected the law in equal numbers, a rarity here.

News analysts, non-governmental organizations and representatives of international institutions were openly disappointed. "Montenegro remains the only country in the region with the law on conflict of interest in accordance neither with the similar laws in the countries of the Region, nor with the EU standards," said a press release by the

United Nations Development Program.

In fact, the existing conflict of interest law allows parliamentarians and delegates to make extra income by managing state companies and doesn't penalize them for failing to report the extra income. Some officials even declare these second jobs, which often produce payouts three to five times higher than their salaries, as part of their public obligation.

One such official, opposition leader Dragan Soc, severely criticized a proposal to stiffen penalties for officials who flaunted the law. Soc is among the 25 percent of officials who reported their income and property for 2005 in August, five months after the official deadline. Soc was caught in a scandal five years ago when, as justice minister, he arranged a supply of computer equipment for his ministry against regulations. Parliament refused the state prosecutors' request to remove Soc from immunity.

Parliament also refused the prosecutor's request to revoke immunity for opposition representative and former President of Parliament Vesna Perovic. Perovic is suspected of demanding a "donation" of about 84 million dinars (US$1.27 million) from a Russian/Montenegrin firm as part of a deal with a municipality where her political party dominated.

Parliament has similarly protected current Health Minister Miodrag Pavlicic. Prosecutors have waited more than a year for Parliament to implement their request to revoke Pavlicic's immunity. Pavlicic is suspected of violating the law on public procurement by enabling a Swiss consulting firm to make an extra profit of more than 8.4 million dinars (US$127,229). His predecessor, Zarko Micovic, is also accused of misusing

MONTENEGRO

The Global Integrity Index:
How effective are the Republic of Motenegro's anti-corruption safeguards?

OVERALL RATING

Very Weak (58)

CATEGORY RATINGS

1) Civil Society, Public Information & Media — Moderate (73)

2) Elections — Very Weak (48)

3) Government Accountability — Very Weak (51)

4) Administration & Civil Service — Very Weak (48)

5) Oversight & Regulation — Weak (66)

6) Anti-Corruption & Rule of Law — Weak (60)

(Scores range from 0 to 100)

The Global Integrity Index, through the Integrity Indicators, assesses the existence and effectiveness of national anti-corruption mechanisms. It does not measure corruption itself (which is nearly impossible). Instead, the Index analyzes the opposite of corruption: the institutions and practices that promote more accountable government and prevent, deter or punish corruption.

The Index is based on nearly 300 Integrity Indicators, discrete scores assigned by local experts using a consistent methodology and scoring criteria for each country. These results are then blindly peer reviewed at the local and international level to ensure consistency and accuracy.

All of the more than 11,000 Integrity Indicator scores that comprise the 2006 Index are published—along with extensive commentary, references and critical peer review comments and perspectives—in the annual Global Integrity Report.

For full results and downloadable datasets, see the Global Integrity website (www.globalintegrity.org).

international donations: He was charged in spring 2005 after a three-year investigation, but the trial has yet to begin.

The influential government officials in charge of the privatization process—Privatization Council Vice President Veselin Vukotic and Branko Vujovic, director of an agency overseeing economic restructuring and foreign investment—are still awaiting trial for illegitimately choosing an adviser in the privatization of a company that monopolized the oil derivates trade, as well as concessions on oil and natural gas research in the Montenegrin part of the Adriatic Sea. The privatization contract was worth more than 252 million dinars (US$3.8 million).

This is the only privatization scandal to reach the courts so far, although the media and non-governmental organizations have repeatedly pointed out the numerous irregularities around the privatization of big public companies.

Montenegrins accept that local judiciary systems are riddled with corruption: Even judges and legal authorities speak of it openly.

"The fact is that there is no case of corruption in the judiciary ending with a verdict. But that can be no longer the only indicator of this phenomenon in Montenegro," said Zoran Pazin, president of the regional court in Podgorica.

Criticism of the judiciary by State Prosecutor Vesna Medenica and Montenegrin police officials garnered much attention in 2006. They reproached judiciary representatives for "devolving their work and disabling the rule of law" by dragging out investigations for several years. Medenica said the court deferred her demand for an investigation of 23

MONTENEGRO

people reportedly responsible for 252 million dinars (US$ 3.8 million) worth of crimes for two years.

Police point to data showing increased arrests as evidence of their commitment to fighting corruption. In most of the 1,800 felonies the department reportedly prosecuted in 2005, "We note elements of corruption," said a police official. Many police say they believe an anti-corruption action plan referred to the government for adoption in June 2006 will help, although experts warn implementation might take years.

Until then, "big corruption" fills the headlines of the local newspapers. The investigation of the state airline was a major story in 2006: Two officials' abuse of their positions allegedly caused more than 840 million dinars (US$12 million) in damages to the company and state. Almost no one pays attention to "small corruption." Smuggled cigarettes are still freely sold on the streets at an estimated tax loss to the state of 3.36 billion dinars to 6.73 billion dinars (US$50.9 million to US$102 million) per year. Customs officials and police are too busy blaming each other to crack down on trade.

Yet "small corruption" pervades daily life. Every third kilowatt of electricity delivered to consumers by the state remains unpaid. Some companies and households haven't paid electricity bills for years in exchange for giving a local politician their votes. Many tourists visiting Montenegro stay at buildings that are not registered as guest accommodations so their owners don't have to pay taxes. Inspectors close their eyes in exchange for bribes of 4,200 dinars (US$64) and up, depending on the size of the building and number of guests.

In the education system, grades are bought and sold.

Medical patients must "treat" the doctor before any treatment, regardless of health insurance. Special care during childbirth costs 42,000 dinars ($US636), while surgeons get 42,000 dinars to 126,000 dinars (US$636 to US$1,900) for more complicated operations. Sometimes a bribe is necessary just to get a bed in a hospital room. Drivers offer bribes of 840 dinars to 1680 dinars (US$13 to US$26) to traffic police to avoid charges. Traffic policemen reported attempted briberies twice this summer, but the defendants in both cases were foreign tourists.

Development corruption is particularly pernicious, but no cases have been proven in court. Many of the country's poor build suburban houses without proper construction permits. Huge business centers, housing complexes and seaside hotels also are erected without permits. It is not unusual for local officials to formally open public facilities without building or use permits. Even the Ministry of Environmental Protection and Urban Planning is located in an illegally-constructed building. The developer sold the space to the government, then built a structure that exceeded the lot's dimensions by several thousand square meters—without consequence.

For an alternative perspective, read the critical peer review commentary on this notebook, part of the 2006 Global Integrity Report (www.globalintegrity.org).

MONTENEGRO

Mozambique:
The Empty Courtroom
By Marcelo Mosse

Corruption in Mozambique is made possible by the very nature of the Mozambican state, where the power of the ruling party overlaps with the state machinery. Despite massive fraud, especially in the privatization process, no senior government representative has ever been convicted, so corruption continues with impunity. In this small African country, pledges to strengthen transparency and integrity are easier said than done.

The history of how Mozambique's political elites have enriched themselves has been amply documented. It essentially resulted from the country's calamitous privatization projects and the squandering of bank resources. More than 10.4 trillion meticais (US$400 million) disappeared from the banking system in the 1990s. The state was forced to repay the money.

One of the most notorious cases involved the 444 billion meticais (US$17 million) Treasury loan to Portuguese businessman Antonio Simões in 1992. Simões received the loan to modernize the Mozambique Steel Company (CSM —*Companhia Siderúrgica de Moçambique*), as well as the wire-drawing company Trefil (*Companhia Moçambicana de Trefilarias*). However, the steel company only operated for a few months after its privatization, as Simões failed to import the raw materials needed or pay salaries. Public authorities never explained the collapse. A 2004 report from Mozambique's Administrative Court to the Parliament claimed that aid from Japan and the U.S. Agency for International Development—distributed by the African Development Bank and the World Bank—went to Mozambican companies without public tender or guarantees for reimbursement.

Allegations of corruption also come from foreign companies trying to invest in the country. For example, following the approval in December 2005 of a new procurement law, a French scanner-production company complained that a contract had been manipulated. Although customs authorities denied any corruption, the damage was done: Mozambique gained the reputation of a country manipulated by political elites. And the reputation is not undeserved. External investors are often forced to give shares and partnerships to ministers in exchange for license approvals. This deters internal, as well as external investment and limits commercial development. Alice Mabote, leader of the NGO Humans Rights League, said Mozambique's problems stem from the lack of accountability practices, particularly in the Parliament, which provides an incentive for corruption.

Corruption does not only flourish at the highest political

MOZAMBIQUE

The Global Integrity Index:
How effective are Mozambique's
anti-corruption safeguards?

OVERALL RATING

Weak (60)

CATEGORY RATINGS

1) Civil Society, Public Information & Media — Weak (67)

2) Elections — Very Weak (45)

3) Government Accountability — Weak (60)

4) Administration & Civil Service — Very Weak (52)

5) Oversight & Regulation — Weak (67)

6) Anti-Corruption & Rule of Law — Weak (69)

(Scores range from 0 to 100)

The Global Integrity Index, through the Integrity Indicators, assesses the existence and effectiveness of national anti-corruption mechanisms. It does not measure corruption itself (which is nearly impossible). Instead, the Index analyzes the opposite of corruption: the institutions and practices that promote more accountable government and prevent, deter or punish corruption.

The Index is based on nearly 300 Integrity Indicators, discrete scores assigned by local experts using a consistent methodology and scoring criteria for each country. These results are then blindly peer reviewed at the local and international level to ensure consistency and accuracy.

All of the more than 11,000 Integrity Indicator scores that comprise the 2006 Index are published—along with extensive commentary, references and critical peer review comments and perspectives—in the annual Global Integrity Report.

For full results and downloadable datasets, see the Global Integrity website (www.globalintegrity.org).

levels in Mozambique, it also grows through bribes paid to traffic police, hospital workers and the sexual extortion that takes place in schools. Former Beira municipality Mayor Chivavice Muchangage reportedly used state facilities for self-enrichment. Two studies on the perception of corruption have been conducted in Mozambique during the past five years.

The first study, by the anti-corruption watchdog Ética Mozambique, surveyed a sample of 1,200 individuals in the provinces of Maputo, Sofala and Nampula. It revealed that one in five respondents paid between 20 and 100 percent of the per capita GDP in bribes.

The 2005 National Research on Governance and Corruption study, which had a larger sample size, revealed that negative perceptions of corruption persisted. The study showed that 28 percent of public workers considered the level of corruption in the Mozambique government to be "very high." Traffic police, who frequently stop motorists to de-mand bribes of 1.3 million meticais (US$50), were named the most dishonest institution.

"Why do people become corrupt?" asked Joana Pelem-be, a nurse in Maputo Central Hospital. "I live in the suburbs and have four children. Two of them study in the city. Three of us need money for the bus every day, but my salary is only 1.6 million meticais (US$61). By the middle of the month, that money no longer exists. Now I ask: Do you think I can refuse the money offered?"

A laboratory technician, Moisés Langa, presented the following argument: "Sometimes others give money as a way of thanking our kindness and good treatment. For me, it does not constitute corruption."

Doctors are not exempt from this behavior. Some use public facilities for their own benefit, for example to see patients from their private clinics.

Assessments of the judicial system paint a gloomy picture. Judges are paid to fix sentences, lawyers bribe clerks to advance a case, and prosecutors are paid to alter the course of an investigation. José Caldeira, one of most prominent lawyers in Mozambique, said that the credibility of the system of justice has been severely eroded by corrupt practices.

The problem is not a lack of laws, but that the laws are not applied. With the political liberalization of the 1990s, the state has taken steps toward redesigning the institutional framework, which could enhance its capacity for controlling corruption. Laws have been passed in an effort to guard against the use of state assets and official posts for personal gain, as well as to establish basic rules for transparency and the declaration of personal assets. However, none of these laws were enforced until 2006. The government approved an anti-corruption strategy this year, but there have been no signs of its implementation.

Ética Mozambique's Abdul Carimo said the country's legal framework, a fundamental instrument for fighting corruption, still needs improvement. Despite the media's repeated publication of the details of corruption scandals, Mozambique doesn't have a record of prosecutions. Ética Mozambique recently finished a project that recorded experiences of corruption by ordinary citizens. In the last six months, Ética received information on 28 cases of corruption and transferred them to the Justice Department, but only one has gone to trial. "It's frustrating," Carimo said.

For an alternative perspective, read the critical peer review commentary on this notebook, part of the 2006 Global Integrity Report (www.globalintegrity.org).

MOZAMBIQUE

Nepal:
Short Memories
By Hari Bahadur Thapa

It took just nine months in jail for former Prime Minister Sher Bahadur Deuba to whitewash his tainted image as the most notoriously corrupt politician in post-democracy Nepal.

On July 26, 2005, the powerful Royal Commission for Corruption Control (RCCC) sentenced Deuba to two years in jail. Deuba was found guilty of taking bribes while granting a road construction project to a favored contractor.

The controversial RCCC, formed by Nepal's absolute ruler King Gyanendra, was later declared illegal by the Supreme Court and shut down, which came as a blessing for Deuba. He emerged as a victim of the king's authoritarian rule and people forgot his murky history.

Deuba, who has been Nepal's prime minister three times, has a long history of allegations. He has been accused of "buying" parliamentarians to sway their vote in his favor, taking hefty commissions to grant projects and massive misuse of the state coffers. Deuba's tale is a classic story of his time, as Nepal pulls away from authoritarianism and returns to democratic rule. Against the backdrop of these transitions, the accused finds it all too easy to slip away from justice.

Deuba escaped prosecution on a technicality. Because the RCCC was an illegal commission set up by the king during his rule, it was easy for Deuba to whip up public sympathy and opposition to the RCCC. The commission was recast as the king's tool to persecute the people who opposed him, rather than to punish corrupt officials.

Not everyone could use the unpopular RCCC as a scapegoat, however. Other officials were accused and investigated by the Commission for Investigation of Abuse of Authority (CIAA). Unlike the king's RCCC, the CIAA was formed in 1990 and is considered a legitimate institution by the people and political parties.

One of the accused, Chiranjivi Wagle, was found guilty and sentenced by the Special Court for illegally accumulating assets worth 27 million Nepalese rupees (US$ 364,707). The law is clear that his sentence carries a mandatory jail term, yet Wagle managed to avoid any time in prison. Wagle's case is not uncommon. Currently, four former ministers who worked under Deuba are facing charges in the courts "for collecting huge amount of property by misusing their positions."

Corruption is rampant in Nepal. With enforcement so lax, corruption becomes a matter of economics. On one side, there is a decreasing fear of accountability among officials. On the opposite side are the substantial rewards corruption offers. There are few risks but high gains.

Since the restoration of the multi-party democracy in

NEPAL

The Global Integrity Index:
How effective are Nepal's anti-corruption safeguards?

OVERALL RATING
Very Weak (50)

CATEGORY RATINGS

1) Civil Society, Public Information & Media — Very Weak (51)

2) Elections — Very Weak (47)

3) Government Accountability — Very Weak (54)

4) Administration & Civil Service — Very Weak (32)

5) Oversight & Regulation — Very Weak (54)

6) Anti-Corruption & Rule of Law — Weak (61)

(Scores range from 0 to 100)

The Global Integrity Index, through the Integrity Indicators, assesses the existence and effectiveness of national anti-corruption mechanisms. It does not measure corruption itself (which is nearly impossible). Instead, the Index analyzes the opposite of corruption: the institutions and practices that promote more accountable government and prevent, deter or punish corruption.

The Index is based on nearly 300 Integrity Indicators, discrete scores assigned by local experts using a consistent methodology and scoring criteria for each country. These results are then blindly peer reviewed at the local and international level to ensure consistency and accuracy.

All of the more than 11,000 Integrity Indicator scores that comprise the 2006 Index are published—along with extensive commentary, references and critical peer review comments and perspectives—in the annual Global Integrity Report.

For full results and downloadable datasets, see the Global Integrity website (www.globalintegrity.org).

the country in 1990, the independent anti-corruption body the Commission for the Investigation of the Abuse of Authority (CIAA) has been active, but not always effective. The CIAA has been willing to confront high-level government officials and political figures. In 2004/2005 it filed 113 cases in pursuit of a total of 1.7 billion rupees (US$23 million) embezzled from the government. But during the king's direct rule between February 2005 and April 2006, the CIAA was swept aside, even after the rival RCCC was dissolved by the Supreme Court.

Ironically the king, who repeatedly preached about fighting corruption, did not need to look far to find it. Indeed, his personal record is dismal. The king consistently spent far more money than allocated on luxuries. He bought cars from Jaguar and Rolls Royce and took lavish vacations. According to Finance Minister Ram Sharan Mahat, in May 2006 the king spent 268 million rupees (US$3.5 million) on several African safaris and Asian trips using the state-run airline's jet. The king traveled with as many as 58 people in his entourage. His son, Paras, also spent lavishly on trips to Europe, Japan, Thailand and the Middle East. Paras once spent 42 million rupees (US$560,000) to take two rhinos as a gift to an Austrian zoo.

As if the perks were not enough, the king also increased his annual salary from 120 million rupees (US$1.6 million) to a whopping 750 million rupees (US$10 million).

Devendra Raj Panday Ph.D., a respected economist, said there was no division between the king's expenses and the state's. Under his direct rule, the king could have taken as

NEPAL

much as he needed with no questions asked and without any risk of the accounts being audited.

"This was an example of capturing entire state by a ruler. His coup was not just aimed at capturing political powers but also the state's financial resources," Panday said.

Kishor Nepal, editor of Nepal magazine, put it this way: "In autocratic rule, corruption is beyond imagination. If his direct rule had not ended we would never have learned the extent of his corruption."

The king's ambition was not limited to money. He sought legitimacy and power as well. On Feb. 8, 2006 the king held municipal elections, which were widely boycotted by the major political parties and groups. The elections cost 240 million rupees (US$3.2 million)—a price that even some of the king's donors found unnecessary.

The king is also accused of creating new agencies and bodies that consolidated his grip on power and spread his network to the grassroots level. These institutions were accountable only to the king. According to a Home Ministry official, who refused to be named because of fear of recrimination, 54 million rupees (US$720,000) were spent for this purpose, which he termed as "as wasteful as pouring water on sand."

During the last five months of the king's rule, then Home Minister Kamal Thapa spent 60 million rupees (US$800,000) cracking down on demonstrations and protests against the king. Information Minister Sirish Sumshere Rana alone distributed 25 million rupees (US$330,000) for this purpose. Since the restoration of democratic rule, there has been no action taken against Thapa or anyone in the king's government who misused state funds.

In April 2006, weeks of pro-democracy protests forced King Gyanendra to give up the power he seized in 2005. He was stripped of his authoritarian rule, as well as his official immunity from prosecution. The king also was forced to reinstate the Parliament, which was dissolved in 2002. Nepal has been without a working Parliament—and therefore any sort of representative bodies, including on the local level—since 2002.

Since the Parliament was reinstated, there has been cause for hope. Elected representatives now hold real power and have moved to restrict the king. For the first time in the monarchy's 237-year history, the income of the royal family is taxed. Furthermore, the property owned by the king, including his palaces and jungles, will also be taxed. The February 2005 election has been invalidated and electoral commission officials behind it have been forced to quit.

But the newly restored government has its hands full. Despite criticism from all sectors, the government has been unable to challenge spending by the army, whose budget increased significantly during the past few years while it was engaged in fighting Maoist rebels.

Several parliamentary committees are actively investigating corruption cases. As the Parliament fights corruption, it may have more experience with the issue than anyone would like to admit. Chiranjivi Wagle, who was convicted of embezzlement by the Supreme Court, has been restored to his seat along with the rest of the Parliament.

For an alternative perspective, read the critical peer review commentary on this notebook, part of the 2006 Global Integrity Report (www.globalintegrity.org).

NEPAL

Nicaragua:
Collision Course

By Camilo de Castro

Carlos Roiz and Ernesto Cantillano died instantly on the night of December 11, 2005. As Carlos Cantillano turned left at a green light, a sport utility vehicle traveling more than 100 miles an hour crashed into his car. Witnesses rushed to the scene. The driver of the SUV and his companion emerged from the vehicle nervous but unscathed. By the time emergency workers arrived, the two men were nowhere to be found.

Some hours later a man was arrested, brought into a police station in Managua and charged with the manslaughter of Ernesto Cantillano and Carlos Roiz. The problem: witnesses did not recognize him as the driver of the SUV. Meanwhile, Francisco Lopez, treasurer of the Sandinista National Liberation Front (FSLN—*Frente de Sandinista Liberación Nacional*) had removed the cars from the scene of the accident. The man that witnesses say is the real driver—Rafael Ortega-Murrillo, the son of former FSLN President Daniel Ortega—had vanished.

In an attempt to cover up the real identity of the driver, police authorities and prosecutors made up witnesses, tainted evidence and orchestrated a carefully prearranged trial, which convicted someone who was never at the scene of the accident. A journalist, who had recognized Ortega-Murrillo as the driver of the SUV, refused to testify out of fear of retaliation.

Despite organizing public protests, there was little the families of the victims could do. Powerful politicians, bent on protecting their political interests, controlled the Nicaraguan judicial system.

"This shows that the courts are controlled by corrupt politicians," said William Roiz, father of Carlos Roiz, "we need to fight to unseat the members of the pact between the FSLN and the PLC [*Partido Liberal Constitucionalista*— Constitutional Liberal Party.]"

Just five months before he leaves office, President Enrique Bolaños faces the lowest popularity rate of any outgoing president in the last 16 years, with almost 50 percent of Nicaraguans disapproving of the way he is handling his job. This result stands in stark contrast to the favorable ratings he received in March of 2003 when he stood before television cameras to denounce acts of corruption during the administration of Arnoldo Aleman (1998-2002).

In a dramatic address to the nation, Bolaños explained how the former president, close associates and family members diverted more than one 1.7 billion córdobas (US$100 million) in public funds to banks in Panama, the United States and the Caribbean.

The accusations began an intense legal battle to bring

The Global Integrity Index:
How effective are Nicaragua's anti-corruption safeguards?

OVERALL RATING

Weak (62)

CATEGORY RATINGS

1) Civil Society, Public Information & Media — Moderate (73)

2) Elections — Very Weak (57)

3) Government Accountability — Very Weak (73)

4) Administration & Civil Service — Very Weak (70)

5) Oversight & Regulation — Weak (65)

6) Anti-Corruption & Rule of Law — Moderate (74)

(Scores range from 0 to 100)

The Global Integrity Index, through the Integrity Indicators, assesses the existence and effectiveness of national anti-corruption mechanisms. It does not measure corruption itself (which is nearly impossible). Instead, the Index analyzes the opposite of corruption: the institutions and practices that promote more accountable government and prevent, deter or punish corruption.

The Index is based on nearly 300 Integrity Indicators, discrete scores assigned by local experts using a consistent methodology and scoring criteria for each country. These results are then blindly peer reviewed at the local and international level to ensure consistency and accuracy.

All of the more than 11,000 Integrity Indicator scores that comprise the 2006 Index are published—along with extensive commentary, references and critical peer review comments and perspectives—in the annual Global Integrity Report.

For full results and downloadable datasets, see the Global Integrity website (www.globalintegrity.org).

the former president to justice, which left Bolaños without the support of the PLC, the political party that brought him to power. Although the FSLN, the main opposition party led by former President Daniel Ortega, initially supported the president's battle against corruption, a series of clashes between Ortega and Bolaños led to a break between the two leaders. After Aleman was sentenced to 20 years house arrest for corruption charges brought against him by a FSLN judge, the terms of his imprisonment became the basis for political negotiations between the FSLN and the PLC in the National Assembly. For the FSLN, the president's loss of support in the National Assembly became an opportunity to strengthen its control over important government institutions. For its part, the PLC sought to negotiate the approval of an amnesty law that would absolve all politicians involved in acts of corruption since 1990 from prosecution. Enrique Quiñonez, leader of the PLC in the National Assembly, insisted that the law would guarantee Nicaragua much needed political stability.

Far from guaranteeing political stability, the amnesty law was further evidence of many legislators' fondness for immunity. Politicians who owe their careers to the head of their political party have few incentives to be accountable to the electorate. The National Assembly runs up debts every year. In addition to a salary of 84,265 córdobas (US$4,750) a month, each legislator receives numerous other privileges: 390,280 córdobas (US$22,000) per year to spend on social projects, 200 gallons of gasoline per month and a tax exemption to import two new cars during his or her term.

The 93 legislators are required to submit a detailed

NICARAGUA

report of expenditures for the social projects they sponsor, but each year only a handful of them comply. Even though the number of staffers hired by the National Assembly tripled since 2002, legislators have only approved 10 laws during the first three months of 2005—most of them of minor relevance. Moreover, according to Roger Arteaga, the director general of Nicaragua's tax collection agency, a substantial number of National Assembly members have not paid taxes since 2001. In response to pressure from the tax collection agency, legislators reduced the funding for the agency by almost 36 million córdobas (US$2 million) in 2005. So far they have not paid their back taxes.

Despite a pattern of questionable behavior, the PLC and FSLN approved a wide range of constitutional reforms in early 2005, ostensibly to make public services more efficient by bringing them under the control of the legislative branch. By placing the administration of telecommunication, electricity and water services under a single institution, known as the Superintendence of Public Services, legislators claimed they would be able to lower costs and provide better, more efficient services. However, the reforms unleashed a grave institutional crisis when the president refused to cede control over the administration of public services.

When the PLC and FSLN appointed loyal partisan bureaucrats to take over government departments, the president sent riot police to prevent them from occupying their offices. Shortly afterwards, the Supreme Court struck down a presidential appeal to declare the constitutional reforms illegal and gave control of government bank accounts to administrators appointed by the National Assembly. In the next seven months, many dollars would be spent to set up the new administrative offices. The director of the newly formed Superintendence of Public Services, Victor Guerrero, hired his son and two other family members as highly paid consultants, while dozens of members of the FSLN and PLC occupied lower administrative positions.

In October, as a result of popular protests and international pressure, the executive and legislative branch struck a deal to suspend the constitutional reforms until Jan. 10, 2007 when the next freely elected president is due to take office. After a prolonged crisis, smaller political parties gained support by denouncing the instability created by the political pact between the FSLN and the PLC. Consequently, just four months before the national elections in November 2006, the FSLN offered to introduce a law to abolish the constitutional reforms approved in January of 2005. Miraculously, the reforms are no longer needed.

The dramatic increase in the international price of oil, however, means huge losses for small and middle size businesses. In part because of poor incentives in the energy sector and repeated political crisis, large swathes of the country currently face prolonged blackouts with no end in sight. Although Nicaragua has an enormous potential for producing renewable energy, foreign investors have been slow to arrive in the country, in part because of lack of trust in the judicial system, which has also been badly undermined by the political pact between the FSLN and the PLC.

"These are long term projects, which require political

stability and clear rules of the game," said Erwin Kruger, president of the Chamber of Private Enterprise.

Investors are not the only ones with misgivings about the judicial system. Recently published polls reveal that the judicial branch is one of the least trusted institutions in government. The courts are frequently implicated in new corruption scandals and judicial decisions are the subject of constant scrutiny by journalists and independent analysts.

Even judges admit that the judicial system needs reform. In a recent report financed by the European Union, 59 percent of the judges, lawyers and public defendants said that the courts lack independence. Another 46 percent said they believe that the courts are corrupt and a solid majority—64 percent—said that the courts do not have enough resources to do their jobs properly.

With salaries that range from 13,820 córdobas to 35,214 córdobas (US$779 to US$1,985) per month, judges are easy targets for bribery. As the judicial system creaks under the strain of a vast backlog, the best way to expedite judicial proceedings is to make payments under the table. Poorer Nicaraguans who cannot make these payments often wait years for a hearing in the courts.

Additionally, Supreme Court justices have become involved in high profile cases of corruption. During last two years, the National Assembly confirmed PLC and FSLN judges to the court as part of a power sharing agreement between Aleman and Ortega. According to the agreement, the presidency of the court would alternate yearly between each party.

Under the presidency of PLC judge Manuel Martinez in 2005, US$609,000 (about 10.8 million córdobas) confiscated from Colombian drug traffickers disappeared from a Supreme Court bank account. The morning of the Sept. 28, 2005, Mario Roberto Peña, a former Nicaraguan public prosecutor wanted for embezzlement in the United States, his son and a substitute judge walked into a bank and withdrew the money with a check signed by Martinez.

More than a year later, it is clear that judges at all levels of the judicial system participated in a scheme to free Colombian drug trafficker Luis Angel Gonzalez Largo, along with his girlfriend and other accomplices. Gonzalez was ultimately extradited to the United States, but no one knows where the money ended up. Far from being reprimanded for the scandal, the Supreme Court justices involved were reappointed for another term, fomenting a culture of impunity within the judicial system.

Several lower court justices are now under investigation for setting drug traffickers free, while high-ranking law enforcement officials warn that Nicaragua is on the verge of becoming a safe heaven for South American drug cartels.

The media continues to play a critical role by reporting cases of wrongdoing by public officials, making the need for transparency and accountability a key issue in the upcoming presidential elections. If it were not for the media, corruption scandals in the judicial system would go unnoticed. In fact, as the theft of US$609,000 from a Supreme Court bank account made headlines, Supreme Court justices silently waited for the scandal to blow over. But insistent media reporting forced

NICARAGUA

the judges to admit wrongdoing—and gave civil society advocates demanding greater transparency more traction in the fight against corruption.

After months of consultation among experts and media groups, a coalition of NGOs drafted an access to information law. It is currently awaiting approval in the National Assembly. Legislators pledged to bring the law to a vote before the end of 2006, but they have yet to include it in the legislative agenda.

Meanwhile, the executive branch began a pilot project, known as Voluntary Strategy of Access to Information (EVA—*Estrategia Voluntaria de Acceso a Informacion*), to provide information about key government ministries via the Web. On the EVA websites citizens can access information about government expenditures, specific projects under execution, and the government officials responsible for them. Even if access to the Internet is still limited, the project sets a valuable precedent.

At the same time, a recent World Bank-financed, nationwide study of the public perception of corruption suggests that efforts to reduce corruption at the local level are paying off. According to the study, between 2003 and 2006 the number of inappropriate payments given to public officials in exchange for services or to avoid fines went down in four out of five of the institutions under review.

The incidence of inappropriate payment in public health clinics declined from 17 to 11 percent, while inappropriate payments in the police force fell from 28 to 18 percent.

Progress was more modest in the public school system, with a decrease of four percentage points in three years, to 53 percent in 2006. The only institution that did not show any improvement at all was the judicial system: In the case of the courts located in Managua, inappropriate payments skyrocketed from 27 percent in 2003 to 42 percent in 2006.

Overall, though, the World Bank's data show that the level of public trust in the government's fight against corruption increased slightly during the last three years.

As the November 2006 presidential and congressional elections come to a head, candidates for public office are making the fight against corruption a key campaign promise. Actions, however, speak louder than words. Despite pressure from civil society organizations demanding greater transparency during the campaign, only one political party has made public the identities of its campaign donors. All of the presidential candidates publicly declared their personal patrimony before the comptrollers office, but the media must work to verify the accuracy of the information. There is already strong evidence that the patrimony declaration made by former President Daniel Ortega, who is running for office for the fifth time, considerably underestimates his personal wealth.

In the end, the future of the fight against corruption is in the hands of Nicaraguans themselves. They must decide among politicians who have repeatedly put their personal interests before the interests of the nation on the one hand, and leaders who are trying to change, little by little, a culture of minimal accountability, nepotism and disregard of the rule of law.

For an alternative perspective, read the critical peer review commentary on this notebook, part of the 2006 Global Integrity Report (www.globalintegrity.org).

NICARAGUA

Nigeria:
Slaying the Sacred Cows
By Akin Olaniyan

Escaping the world of "unofficial charges" is difficult,
if not impossible, for the average Nigerian. Almost everyone
pays bribes on some level: Professionals, politicians and even
youth are wrapped up in a system estimated to have cost
Nigeria more than 12 trillion naira (US$100 billion) in illicit
money transfers alone.

After the embarrassing disclosure that the late military
ruler Sani Abacha and his close aides looted the treasury of
282 billion naira (US$2.2 billion)—this in a country where
an estimated 70 percent of the population live on less than
128 naira (US$1) a day—it looked like Nigerians were finally
determined to confront corruption.

The decision to deal with the problem won praise at home
and abroad. Due diligence initiatives have saved government
funds, while fiscal responsibility laws and the establishment
of budget and planning offices at the ministry of finance show
promise. The Economic and Financial Crimes Commission

(EFCC), under the leadership of Mallam Nuhu Ribadu, won respect by arresting previously untouchable Nigerians.

But seven years into President Olusegun Obasanjo's government, doubts remain as to the anti-corruption campaign's effectiveness. The unexpected reassignment of widely respected Finance Minister Ngozi Okonjo-Iweala and her subsequent resignation from the cabinet raised questions about the government's commitment to accountability. Perhaps most importantly, one still has the impression that Nigerians are willing to take risks at even the smallest chance to make fast money.

Such was the conclusion I reached after a run-in with police in April 2006. It was mid-morning on a Saturday and I was driving to a shopping complex on Victoria Island off the capital city of Lagos. Realizing too late that I had driven past the complex, I turned and headed back, only to be stopped by a one-armed policeman. My offense: driving against traffic on a one-way road, for which offenders are fined 25,000 naira (about US$193). As usual, the fine was negotiable. I was allowed to go without a bribe, having identified myself as a journalist, but as I drove back home I was reminded that those who fight corrupt practices have their work cut out for them.

When I needed a new car, like most Nigerians who cannot afford new ones, I hired a car dealer to go across the border to Benin to arrange the purchase of a used car for me. His charges included a fee to pay a customs official to escort the car into Nigeria. Registering the car followed a similar pattern. For a premium on the official license fee of 2,000 naira (US$15), I could get my registration the same day, compared to a wait of three days to a week. Call it a gift or bribe:

NIGERIA

The Global Integrity Index:
How effective are Nigeria's anti-corruption safeguards?

OVERALL RATING

Moderate (75)

CATEGORY RATINGS

1) Civil Society, Public Information & Media — Very Weak (57)

2) Elections — Moderate (73)

3) Government Accountability — Moderate (70)

4) Administration & Civil Service — Strong (85)

5) Oversight & Regulation — Strong (80)

6) Anti-Corruption & Rule of Law — Strong (84)

(Scores range from 0 to 100)

The Global Integrity Index, through the Integrity Indicators, assesses the existence and effectiveness of national anti-corruption mechanisms. It does not measure corruption itself (which is nearly impossible). Instead, the Index analyzes the opposite of corruption: the institutions and practices that promote more accountable government and prevent, deter or punish corruption.

The Index is based on nearly 300 Integrity Indicators, discrete scores assigned by local experts using a consistent methodology and scoring criteria for each country. These results are then blindly peer reviewed at the local and international level to ensure consistency and accuracy.

All of the more than 11,000 Integrity Indicator scores that comprise the 2006 Index are published—along with extensive commentary, references and critical peer review comments and perspectives—in the annual Global Integrity Report.

For full results and downloadable datasets, see the Global Integrity website (www.globalintegrity.org).

Nigerians know money works wonders, and in most cases, people choose to pay with few questions asked.

This is certainly the case for Nigerian university students. On most campuses, students who buy books or handouts published by lecturers are guaranteed as much as a 20-point markup on their final examination. Most students simply choose the easier route to good grades.

I myself have faced a frustrating time determining what happened to some 18,000 naira (about US$139) I paid for my electric bill for my three-bedroom apartment between April 2004 and April 2006. The amount is still reflected on current bills as unpaid. I was advised to write to the Power Holding Company of Nigeria (PHCN), but almost 10 months later the officials still couldn't find an explanation, except to say that it was not an uncommon case.

With their high-profile scandals involving enormous amounts of money, one would think common Nigerians were saints compared to government officials. The most significant recent scandal involved President Obasanjo's alleged attempt to induce National Assembly members to extend his term by paying them each 50 million naira (more than US$387,000). Professor Shola Adeyeye, a House of Representatives member from Osun State, insists that the money changed hands, despite strong denials by government officials.

Diepreye Alamieyeseigha, the former governor of Bayelsa State, was arrested by police in London in September 2005 for money laundering offenses and detained for 66 days. Alamieyeseigha's escape and sudden reappearance in the Bayelsa state capital of Yenagoa two months later remains

NIGERIA

as controversial as it was daring. Accused of enriching his immediate family with government funds, he was later removed as governor and is now standing trial in a Nigerian court in an unprecedented case.

The recent arrest and arraignment of two aides for Ekiti State Governor Ayo Fayose on charges of misappropriating 1.25 billion naira (US$9.6 million) from the state's Integrated Poultry Project might lack the drama of the Alamieyeseigha case, but is intriguing nonetheless. The aides, Goke Olatunji and Gbenga James, face 15 counts of money laundering and corrupt enrichment. The governor's fate is unclear. Twenty-four other governors out of 36 have been investigated for similar cases and may be arraigned at the end of their tenure next year, according to the EFCC.

The EFCC chairman said the agency has done its job well, citing as evidence the recovery of some 513 billon naira (US$4 billion) from corrupt officials. Not everyone is impressed, however. General Ishola Williams of Transparency International's Nigeria office said the government cannot win the "war on corruption" It is Nigerian citizens who must be determined to reduce corruption.

"There is an apparent political will: Anti-corruption agencies can bark and bite and they seem to have good leadership," said Williams, but he pointed out that their efforts are undermined by Obasanjo's refusal give the agencies independence or funding, in addition to blocking a freedom of information bill.

Echoing these sentiments, Adeyeye said winning the war against corruption was proving difficult because of reluctance to slay Nigeria's "sacred cows." However, he noted that future administrations might have difficulty rolling back the small gains of the present anti-corruption campaign, such as the Nigeria Extractive Industries Initiative (NEITI). Obasanjo could further lock in these gains by submitting records of oil production and export to parliamentary oversight, Adeyeye said. The chances of that happening, however, are as small as the average Nigerian wage.

For an alternative perspective, read the critical peer review commentary on this notebook, part of the 2006 Global Integrity Report (www.globalintegrity.org).

NIGERIA

Pakistan:
An Unhealthy Politics

By Mahmood Iqbal

The sight of the elderly woman trudging out of the nursery ward at a major public hospital sent shivers down my spine. She was carrying a baby in her arms, followed by another young woman who self-consciously kept adjusting her shawl, trying to conceal her budding womanhood from onlookers.

I overheard them whimpering as they sat on a bench to wrap the baby in a piece of white cloth. "We kept imploring [the doctors] for hours, but nobody bothered to attend to my child," the young mother moaned as tears rolled down her pale cheeks. "It makes no [difference] to them whether you die or survive."

This is Peshawar. It is the capital of Pakistan's North West Frontier Province, a city of no more than three million people, one third of whom are Afghans. The Mutahidda Majlis-i-Amal, a conglomerate of religious parties, has held power in Peshwar since 2002 and claims to champion the cause of humanity.

Initially, I had planned to dig up some high profile story involving the government's shocking negligence in dealing with corruption to file as my Reporter's Notebook. However, the pleading looks of the young mother moved me to focus my attention here, on how corruption brings misery to everyday life.

Hospitals in Pakistan are a bleak example of mismanagement, corruption and above all, flagrant violations of regulations. As usual, a sickening stench greeted me in the hospital's overcrowded corridors. Inside the wards, patients outnumbered the beds. Some rested on benches, while other patients set up their own makeshift beds in the poorly lit corners. Not surprisingly, no senior doctors were available.

"Even in the intensive care unit, I had to run to the medicine shops on the main street and bring simple analgesics for my mother. Can a heart attack wait for you to bring medicines for the patient before it strikes?" said one of my journalist colleagues, whose mother died of cardiac arrest in the same hospital in July.

Similar to all other social and public institutions in Pakistan, the health and education systems are rife with corruption, as well as unsanitary conditions.

"Wherever institutions are weak, corrupt officials are more scared of media than the discipline and regulations of their office," said Mohammed Riaz, a senior journalist at the Dawn, Pakistan's leading newspaper. "The media, too, no doubt, is infested with corruption to its core, but it is still effective to expose the corrupt practices of civil and military bureaucracy."

The government has been touting reforms in the educa-

PAKISTAN

The Global Integrity Index:
How effective are Pakistan's anti-corruption safeguards?

OVERALL RATING

Weak (69)

CATEGORY RATINGS

1) Civil Society, Public Information & Media — Weak (63)

2) Elections — Weak (70)

3) Government Accountability — Very Weak (59)

4) Administration & Civil Service — Weak (62)

5) Oversight & Regulation — Strong (82)

6) Anti-Corruption & Rule of Law — Strong (81)

(Scores range from 0 to 100)

The Global Integrity Index, through the Integrity Indicators, assesses the existence and effectiveness of national anti-corruption mechanisms. It does not measure corruption itself (which is nearly impossible). Instead, the Index analyzes the opposite of corruption: the institutions and practices that promote more accountable government and prevent, deter or punish corruption.

The Index is based on nearly 300 Integrity Indicators, discrete scores assigned by local experts using a consistent methodology and scoring criteria for each country. These results are then blindly peer reviewed at the local and international level to ensure consistency and accuracy.

All of the more than 11,000 Integrity Indicator scores that comprise the 2006 Index are published—along with extensive commentary, references and critical peer review comments and perspectives—in the annual Global Integrity Report.

For full results and downloadable datasets, see the Global Integrity website (www.globalintegrity.org).

tion sector, however, not all strata of the society want to see changes to the status quo.

"The first casualty of the haphazard reforms program was the examination system. Before the reforms, examinations used to be held according to a schedule, but now even institutions fail to know the exact date of examinations," a senior professor at the Peshawar University said.

Senior educators complain that the initiative to bring about changes in the curricula has also proven futile. "The bogey of reforms has derailed whatever flawed system already existed," one said.

A culture of secrecy in the government, a deepening unrest among the people, a mounting wave of militancy, rising incidents of kidnapping and assassinations and most recently, the increasing wave of Talibanization, have all but chilled the already hostile atmosphere in the country.

The recovery of the handcuffed body of kidnapped tribal journalist Hayatullah Khan on June 16, 2006, reinforced the conviction that both official and unofficial regulations exist within the country to restrict the freedom of the press.

No one welcomed the public outcry against this cold-blooded killing more than photojournalist Mukesh Rupeta and his colleague, who had been secretly detained by government intelligence officers in Jacobabad, Sindh for three months.

Pakistani President General Pervez Musharraf, who is also the chief of the army, came to power by removing the elected government of Nawaz Sharif in 1999. He suspended the constitution and began enforcing the Provisional Consti-

PAKISTAN

tutional Order to proclaim his rule and to run the affairs of the country. Subsequently, the Superior Judiciary—under the much-abused doctrine of necessity—legitimized the Musharraf's action.

The overall situation during the past seven years has been marked by violence in the tribal belt of Waziristan, Balochistan and elsewhere in the country. In Waziristan, about 80,000 regular troops are working to eliminate an estimated 300 foreign militants hiding in the area and to restore the rule of law to the volatile region.

In December 2005, the government launched a string of operations against renegade tribal chief Akbar Khan Bugti in Balchistan. Bugti had initiated an armed struggle against the security forces. The reasons for this uprising, according to the Balochi leaders, were the lack of autonomy for Balochistan, unfair access to natural resources and the repressive presence of the army in the province.

An unspecified number of innocent people, among them women and children, have perished in these operations, which has badly hurt the credibility of the armed forces.

Pakistan is a country of contradictions. It has enormous natural and human resources, but it is poverty stricken. Its people are intelligent, warm, hospitable and kind, but they are steeped in corruption.

Pakistan's leading anti-corruption agency, the National Accountability Bureau, has pinpointed the major causes of corruption in the society. These include, among others, flagrant abuse of power, non-compliance with the law, absence of an effective anti-corruption mechanism, political leaders' incompetence, lack of transparency in the government's decision-making process, cumbersome procedures in the executive system and weaknesses in the judicial system. All of these have hindered the development of proper ethical and business standards for the public and private sectors.

The inefficiency of the official machinery was exposed when a powerful earthquake rattled large parts of South Asia on October 8, 2005. The quake flattened thousands of houses in Pakistan, killing at least 70,000 people. More than three million people were rendered homeless.

Despite a huge response by the Pakistanis and the international community to rush relief goods to the areas, survivors complained they that had not received any assistance. They sneered at the official aid distribution channels and relied more on the assistance provided by religious and humanitarian organizations.

"During the whole relief operation, excessive use of helicopters was made, but despite that, stranded people had no shelter or food," said an official in the Provincial Earthquake Rehabilitation Authority, who requested anonymity.

"But on most of the flights, civil and military bureaucrats would have frequent aerial views of the unprecedented destruction," he said. "It was evident from the start of the chopper service that the government could not sustain it for a long time."

With the general elections scheduled for 2007, the opposition parties are flexing their muscles. They are maneuvering to bring a no-confidence vote against the prime minister, who has faced much political fallout since the Supreme Court scrapped

PAKISTAN

the sale of Pakistan Steel Mills after malpractice in the deal was exposed. The court directed that the Council of Common Interests (CCI) be re-instituted to investigate the issue.

Perhaps it should not have bothered. The CCI, in its first meeting after being resurrected, gave a go-ahead decision for the privatization of the steel company, malpractice notwithstanding. The genuine reservations of the stakeholders were barely considered.

Mismanagement, indiscipline and corruption. From the dimly lit hospital wards to the highest council chambers, the story is sadly familiar. It is yet to be seen whether there is light at the end of this tunnel.

For an alternative perspective, read the critical peer review commentary on this notebook, part of the 2006 Global Integrity Report (www.globalintegrity.org).

The Philippines:
Numbers Game

By Sheila Coronel

Every year, during the week before Christmas, small
crowds gather outside the fortress-like home of Rodolfo Pineda, the operator of a vast, illegal gambling network that spans
several provinces of the main Philippine island of Luzon.

Pineda lives in his hometown of Lubao, located in the
heart of the great Central Luzon plain, a 90-minute drive
from Manila. In this sleepy town of rice farmers and assorted
tradespeople, the real power lies not in the whitewashed town
hall or the centuries-old Catholic Church: It resides in the
Pinedas' high-walled, high-security compound. Although the
country's biggest gambling lord is reclusive and rarely seen
in public, his wife Lilia was the town's mayor for nine years.
Their son, Dennis, is the current mayor.

During the Christmas season, all roads in Lubao lead to
the Pinedas. Every day, scores of villagers line up for the bags
of goodies that the family gives away. The town's school-
teachers get a leg of ham, corned beef and other canned

goods. Ordinary folk take home gift bags containing dressed chicken, sardines, rice and noodles.

If anything serves as a metaphor for the depth and breadth of corruption in the Philippines, it is *jueteng*, the illegal numbers game of which Pineda is the biggest operator. The gambling network shows how nearly everyone—from ordinary citizens to public officials and even the so-called guardians of morality and watchdogs of society—is complicit in the corruption that gnaws at the foundations of the country's fragile institutions.

Various estimates put annual revenues from *jueteng* at about 30 billion pesos (US$600 million) a year, almost equal the annual earnings of some of the Philippines' biggest tobacco and telecommunications firms.

Former police officials familiar with jueteng operations say that 20 to 30 percent of this amount—anywhere from six billion pesos (US$120 million) to ten billion pesos (US$200 million)—is paid as bribes or protection money to town mayors, provincial governors, police chiefs, members of Congress, and top-level officers of the Philippine National Police. The Catholic Church and journalists are also among the many beneficiaries of gambling profits, they say.

The movie actor Joseph Estrada, who was elected president in 1998, fell from power in a popular uprising in 2001 because of accusations that he was receiving monthly payoffs from *jueteng* operators, among other issues. A provincial governor, believed to be a *jueteng* lord himself, revealed that he collected money from gambling operators every month, packed the bills in black attaché cases and delivered them to Estrada's home.

Gloria Macapagal-Arroyo succeeded Estrada after the "people power" protests. But she also has been embroiled in a *jueteng* scandal. In 2005, the Senate investigated charges that her husband, brother-in-law and son were taking bribes from gambling lords. Several witnesses in the Senate hearings also alleged that Mrs. Arroyo's 2004 election campaign was partly financed by, among others, the Pinedas.

Jueteng is a form of lottery introduced by Chinese traders to the Philippines at least 100 years ago. The earliest court ruling on it dates back to 1905, when a colonial-era tribunal convicted the owner and financier of a *jueteng* operation. In the 1930s, the grand-uncle of President Arroyo's husband, a provincial governor, was dismissed from his post on charges that he was coddling a *jueteng* lord to raise money for his election.

For generations, illegal gambling and politics have intertwined in the Philippines. Some of the country's most prominent political families, including that of former President Corazon C. Aquino, have been linked to illegal gambling. In most of Luzon, *jueteng* is the lifeblood of local politics. It is the major source of campaign contributions. During elections, the network of bet collectors doubles as a campaign machine.

After elections, local officials use gambling money for patronage. Voters traditionally bring their supplications to politicians who dole out money for hospital bills and school fees, weddings, baptisms and burials, expecting their generosity will be remembered on election day.

Jueteng keeps the police running as well. Because the

PHILLIPINES

The Global Integrity Index:
How effective are the Philippines'
anti-corruption safeguards?

OVERALL RATING
Moderate (73)

CATEGORY RATINGS

1) Civil Society, Public Information & Media — Moderate (72)

2) Elections — Very Weak (60)

3) Government Accountability — Moderate (71)

4) Administration & Civil Service — Moderate (73)

5) Oversight & Regulation — Strong (85)

6) Anti-Corruption & Rule of Law — Moderate (78)

(Scores range from 0 to 100)

The Global Integrity Index, through the Integrity Indicators, assesses the existence and effectiveness of national anti-corruption mechanisms. It does not measure corruption itself (which is nearly impossible). Instead, the Index analyzes the opposite of corruption: the institutions and practices that promote more accountable government and prevent, deter or punish corruption.

The Index is based on nearly 300 Integrity Indicators, discrete scores assigned by local experts using a consistent methodology and scoring criteria for each country. These results are then blindly peer reviewed at the local and international level to ensure consistency and accuracy.

All of the more than 11,000 Integrity Indicator scores that comprise the 2006 Index are published—along with extensive commentary, references and critical peer review comments and perspectives—in the annual Global Integrity Report.

For full results and downloadable datasets, see the Global Integrity website (www.globalintegrity.org).

police are underfunded, protection money is used to buy gasoline for police vehicles, office supplies, even medicine for sick cops. Moreover, *jueteng* is an employment agency giving jobs to some 150,000 bet collectors. Its grassroots base includes millions of poor Filipinos who bet one peso—about two U.S. cents—or more in a game of chance that has deep roots in popular folklore.

Despite the exposés, many Filipinos condone *jueteng* and accept it as a fact of life. In thousands of villages it is considered a popular entertainment and distraction. Bettors make their wagers based on dreams, omens and premonitions. In *jueteng*, numbers take on a mystical quality: the heavens send signs and favor those who read them well.

Although it provides unending fodder for political scandal, those who play the game hardly consider themselves part of a network of organized crime and corruption. *Jueteng*, after all, also serves as a social safety net, funding services that the government, were it not so corrupt, should deliver. The irony is that the government is corrupt precisely because of *jueteng* and similar rackets.

The truth is that illegal gambling preys on the poor, traps them in relationships of patronage and makes them complicit in the structures that oppress them. But it also provides them with temporary relief from their misery. In the process, it corrupts key democratic institutions and processes. Law enforcement, the justice system and elections are compromised by *jueteng* money. In the end, the country sinks deeper and deeper into the corruption mire.

In 2005, the Arroyo government was shaken by the

PHILLIPINES

release of a tape of apparently wiretapped conversations between the president and an election commissioner. The conversations indicated a conspiracy to rig the 2004 vote and set off high-profile investigations on the conduct of the polling that made Mrs. Arroyo president.

One whistleblower said he was present at a dinner for 27 election supervisors at the Arroyo home in January 2004. The president was there, as was Lilia Pineda, widely known as a close friend of the Arroyos. After a meal of black pasta, Pineda supposedly gave each of the election supervisors envelopes containing 25,225 pesos (US$500) in cash.

Other revelations, including accounts of the military allegedly cheating on behalf of Arroyo and presidential relatives receiving bribes from jueteng operators, plunged the presidency into crisis. An impeachment was initiated in 2005, but reached a dead end when the complaint was rejected by a majority in Congress. Because many legislators reportedly received payoffs in exchange for their vote, the process did not clear the president's name, but only muddied it even more.

The crisis has taken its toll on government credibility. The institutions are widely perceived as unable to hold the president or anyone else to account. Polls in 2005 and 2006 showed a palpable increase in public cynicism, with distrust of the presidency, Congress and various executive branch departments on the rise. Most Filipinos did not believe the government was sincere about fighting corruption, according to the polls.

In Lubao, Pineda continues to reign over his gambling empire, accustomed by now to the cycle of Philippine politics: high-profile exposés followed by crackdowns, then business as usual. After all, the Pinedas survived both the both Estrada and Arroyo scandals unscathed. In late 2005, Arroyo herself ordered a crackdown on gambling operations, including Pineda's. The gambling stopped for a few months, as it had when Estrada's *jueteng* links were exposed in 2000. By mid-2006, *jueteng* was back, enjoying the legal and political protection it always has.

For an alternative perspective, read the critical peer review commentary on this notebook, part of the 2006 Global Integrity Report (www.globalintegrity.org).

PHILLIPINES

Romania:
After the Revolution

By Paul Radu

In December 1989, millions of people around the world flipped on their televisions and watched live broadcasts of the popular Romanian uprising—a grassroots revolt that brought down a corrupt and brutish Communist dictatorship and harbingered a new era for the lands behind the Iron Curtain.

It's time to tell the rest of the story.

The fact is that for the 22 million people living in Romania, the troubles are not over. Former agents and informants of the Romanian *Securitate* (secret police) still hold key positions of influence in the government, the judiciary, the media and all areas of public life. Indeed, many individuals responsible for the current high-level corruption scandals in Romania are former *Securitate* officers and Communist regime officials.

Today, some of the same characters that figured so prominently into the Ceaucescu power structure are once again on live TV. But this time they are parading between their fancy mansions and the headquarters of the National Anti-Corruption Directorate (DNA–*Directia Nationala Anticoruptie*) in Bucharest.

Corruption is endemic in Romania. Despite the country's desperate fight to become a member of the European Union in January 2007, one glance at the DNA's Web site highlights the level of corruption. For example, the prime minister of the former Social-Democrat government, now the president of the chamber of deputies, was brought up on corruption charges in 2006. He had company: A deputy prime minister of the government in power, a senator, a high-ranking officer of the Romanian Secret Service, four other members of the Romanian Parliament, two army generals and a number of other government officials were also charged. Their offenses range from the use of their offices against public interest to active and passive corruption.

The 2005 annual report is illustrative: The DNA boasts that out of the 744 defenders sent to trial that year, 127 had positions of power or leadership in the Romanian government.

A number of prominent politicians and public servants —including the current head of state, Traian Basescu—have been the subject of investigations during recent years, and a number of these cases have reached the Romanian courts. However, not one of the high-level Romanian politicians that have been charged has seen jail time.

Usually the accused claim that the corruption investigations are politically motivated. But the latest European Union monitoring report notes that the number and quality of nonpartisan investigations into allegations of high-level corrup-

The Global Integrity Index:
How effective are Romania's anti-corruption safeguards?

OVERALL RATING
Strong (86)

CATEGORY RATINGS

1) Civil Society, Public Information & Media — Strong (84)

2) Elections — Strong (90)

3) Government Accountability — Moderate (78)

4) Administration & Civil Service — Strong (83)

5) Oversight & Regulation — Very Strong (91)

6) Anti-Corruption & Rule of Law — Very Strong (91)

(Scores range from 0 to 100)

The Global Integrity Index, through the Integrity Indicators, assesses the existence and effectiveness of national anti-corruption mechanisms. It does not measure corruption itself (which is nearly impossible). Instead, the Index analyzes the opposite of corruption: the institutions and practices that promote more accountable government and prevent, deter or punish corruption.

The Index is based on nearly 300 Integrity Indicators, discrete scores assigned by local experts using a consistent methodology and scoring criteria for each country. These results are then blindly peer reviewed at the local and international level to ensure consistency and accuracy.

All of the more than 11,000 Integrity Indicator scores that comprise the 2006 Index are published—along with extensive commentary, references and critical peer review comments and perspectives—in the annual Global Integrity Report.

For full results and downloadable datasets, see the Global Integrity website (www.globalintegrity.org).

tion has substantially increased during recent months.

The progress noted by EU officials, however, has yet to be noticed by ordinary Romanians. Despite the much-publicized government crusades against corruption, the latest polls indicate that 48 percent of the population believes the level of corruption not changed since the Liberal-Democrat government took power at the end 2004. Some 24 percent of people said they are convinced that corruption has increased. Only 15 percent of Romanians responded that corruption has diminished.

Corruption has hit ordinary Romanians in the pocketbook, leaving them with one of the lowest monthly wages in Europe. The biggest corruption scandals occurred with the privatization of huge industrial assets, banks and other resources that took place during the past decade. Many of these privatizations were a boon for a handful of well-placed officials in the various post-communist Romanian governments—but were a raw deal for the ordinary Romanian citizens.

The battle over Romania's substantial national resources—including gold, oil and natural gas—fueled high-level corruption and triggered a frantic political fight. One of the biggest scandals involved RAFO, a formerly state-owned oil refinery located in the northeast part of Romania. In 2001, the then-ruling Social Democrat Party awarded the refinery to Corneliu Iacobov, then a branch vice-president. During the following three years, the refinery amassed a crushing debt of 83.6 billion lei (US$29 billion) in unpaid taxes. It was ultimately sold to a British company for an

ROMANIA

undisclosed amount.

I investigated the transaction and proved that the London based company was owned by associates of Iacobov, who were very close to the former Romanian president, Ion Iliescu and to two of his key advisors, a general with the intelligence services and a senator. The latter admitted he was cashing in significant amounts of money from companies involved in the RAFO affair.

The plot thickened when it was revealed that the very same people behind the corrupt RAFO sale were also behind the biggest financial disaster in Romanian history. Bancorex was one of the main state-owned banks when it collapsed under the weight of bad loans paid to politically connected clientele, who never bothered to pay their debts. The collapse resulted in a 55.76 trillion lei loss (US$20 trillion), which was passed on to Romanian taxpayers. The state has yet to cover the debt. Nevertheless, even the former Prime Minister Adrian Nastase is now under investigation on the suspicion that he bought land in the center of Bucharest for far less than its fair market value—from the same group of people involved in the RAFO affair.

The oil wars may come to haunt the current government as well. Calin Popescu Tariceanu, the prime minister of Romania, is implicated in a scandal surrounding Rompetrol, a publicly owned company listed on the Romanian Stock Exchange. The company is being investigated for alleged illegal transactions and unpaid debts to the Romanian Treasury.

Both the Rompetrol and RAFO case are reported on daily by the Romanian news media. But the reporting frequently is biased, depending on the interests of the various media owners. Balanced and fair reporting is rare in Romania. Freelance, independent investigative journalists have a difficult time getting published. I have worked with my colleagues in the Romanian Center for Investigative Journalism on creating a chart depicting media ownership in Romania. We found many examples of biased coverage and that many of the more than 700 Romanian newspapers only defend the business interests of their publishers. The interests of Romanian readers, alas, receive scant consideration.

The apathy is mutual. Readers care little more about newspapers than the publishers do, and so newspaper circulation plummets daily. Ordinary Romanians are far more concerned about getting into the political and economic environment in which corruption is an epidemic.

"We realized that corruption and bribery have become an industry," said Manuela Preoteasa, one of the experts behind the publication of the "2004 Bribery Handbook."

Yes, there is actually a published guide about how to bribe your way around Romania. The handbook not only presents the customary amounts of bribes paid to public servants, but also offers practical tips on how to go about it: "You want to get married and you quickly need the medical certificates proving you are in good health? You go to Miss Flory in this Bucharest clinic and leave your ID and 50 lei (US$18) in an envelope. The next day, in the evening, you pick up the envelope from the same Miss Flory with the certificates and without ever having been examined. It's guaranteed you won't find any sexually transmitted disease

ROMANIA

mentioned in the needed papers!"

Amid the depressing state of affairs though, there are a few glimmers of hope. The Ministry of European Integration has initiated an "Unmask the Bribery Campaign," targeted at the petty corruption and bribery experienced by Romanians on a daily basis. The initiative is meant to educate ordinary citizens. But until Romanians see and feel that justice is being done in the big corruption cases, any initiative targeting petty operators will have limited credibility. Government action against the thus far untouchable empire of graft and embezzlement must go further than splashing pictures on a TV screen.

For an alternative perspective, read the critical peer review commentary on this notebook, part of the 2006 Global Integrity Report (www.globalintegrity.org).

Russian Federation:
For Enemies, the Law

By Galina Stolyarova

The flyers glued to the entrances of the apartment buildings look, at first sight, unremarkable.

These leaflets pasted up in many Russian Federation towns are advertising "draft-dodging" services. They provide a contact number for a shadow firm, holding out the promise that your teenage son can be spared the dreadful fate that would await him in the armed forces—for a hefty fee.

Hundreds of people see these leaflets every day, including, no doubt, law enforcement officers, but they stay up on the walls just the same. In St. Petersburg, the deal is a bargain at 68,000 rubles (US$2,574) while in Moscow the price reaches 172,000 rubles (US$6,436).

As reports of brutal hazing continue to come from every region of the country, many families are looking for an escape route from military service for their children.

The criminal market has responded accordingly. According to Georgy Satarov, director of the Indem Foundation, a

Moscow-based anti-corruption watchdog, the cost of bribing your way out of military service has skyrocketed. It now costs around 20 times more than in 2001, probably a higher rate of inflation than for any other service.

According to Indem, the level of bribes paid to officials by Russian businessmen has grown more than tenfold in the last five years. The average bribe in the commercial sector has increased from 611,384 to 6.5 million rubles (US$22,900 to US$243,750), the survey said.

Fifty-three percent of Russians polled by the nationwide agency VTSIOM said they have paid a bribe at least once in their lives. Nineteen percent of survey's respondents admitted making corrupt payments on a regular basis. Sixty percent of respondents said corruption in Russia is irradicable.

When it comes to planning a child's education and career, corruption begins very early in the process. As well as having to pay a sweetener of up to 27,000 rubles (US$1000) to get a child into kindergarten, Russian parents may well have to fork out 53,396 to 533,960 rubles (US$2,000 to US$20,000) to obtain their child's university entrance.

Not even health care is immune from the cancer of under-the-counter payments. If you fall ill or need an operation, the cost of getting yourself into a well-equipped hospital can be 40,047 to 80,094 rubles (US$1500 to US$3000). And even in the public hospitals used by the poor, money talks.

I have seen penniless old people lying in corridors in Russian clinics, begging for food, while others occupy shabby beds dating from shortly after World War II. They rest without bed linens and, in some cases, even without mattresses. It is an open secret that a backhander of 400 roubles (US$15) per day will get a patient washed, fed and properly looked after.

Half of all bribes in Russia are paid to doctors, and more than 20 percent of Russians have reported not being able to get the treatment they needed because they could not afford the bribe, according to an Indem study.

While corruption scams are booming, the programs meant to combat graft and organized crime don't seem to be making much headway.

During the summer of 2006, in an attempt to fight the illegal alcohol market and to protect people from widely distributed (often poisonous) bootleg liquor, the Russian government introduced a new system of labels for all imported wines and spirits. When the clampdown was supposed to start, too few new excise labels had been printed for the genuine imported wines and spirits. It would take months to deliver them.

The reform clobbered many legal businesses including wine boutiques, wholesale suppliers and restaurants, because the businesses were stuck with thousands of bottles lacking the correct new labels.

President Vladimir Putin has made some strong statements denouncing bribery and corruption. In July 2006 he signed into law a bill ratifying the Council of Europe's Criminal Law Convention on Corruption.

But Putin's words must be weighed carefully against his actions—or the lack of them.

The government's promises to crack down on corruption

RUSSIA

The Global Integrity Index:
How effective are The Russian Federations's anti-corruption safeguards?

OVERALL RATING
Weak (63)

CATEGORY RATINGS

1) Civil Society, Public Information & Media — Weak (60)

2) Elections — Weak (68)

3) Government Accountability — Very Weak (53)

4) Administration & Civil Service — Very Weak (56)

5) Oversight & Regulation — Moderate (73)

6) Anti-Corruption & Rule of Law — Moderate (70)

(Scores range from 0 to 100)

The Global Integrity Index, through the Integrity Indicators, assesses the existence and effectiveness of national anti-corruption mechanisms. It does not measure corruption itself (which is nearly impossible). Instead, the Index analyzes the opposite of corruption: the institutions and practices that promote more accountable government and prevent, deter or punish corruption.

The Index is based on nearly 300 Integrity Indicators, discrete scores assigned by local experts using a consistent methodology and scoring criteria for each country. These results are then blindly peer reviewed at the local and international level to ensure consistency and accuracy.

All of the more than 11,000 Integrity Indicator scores that comprise the 2006 Index are published—along with extensive commentary, references and critical peer review comments and perspectives—in the annual Global Integrity Report.

For full results and downloadable datasets, see the Global Integrity website (www.globalintegrity.org).

have yet to be translated into a coherent policy. Despite ambitious declarations, corruption in Russia is rife. According to the Moscow based National Anti-Corruption Committee, corruption costs Russia $40 billion a year.

Worldwide perceptions of Russia's corruption problems, as tracked by Transparency International (TI), have slid from bad to worse. In TI's Corruption Perceptions Index, Russia plummeted from 71st place in 2002 to 126th in 2005, placing the country alongside Albania and Sierra Leone in the court of public opinion.

To combat corruption effectively, a country needs a free media, a parliament containing something resembling a robust and genuine opposition and unbiased courts. In Russia, since Putin's rise to power, the integrity of each of these institutions has rapidly deteriorated.

All nationwide TV channels are now under state control. Pro-presidential bloc United Russia holds an overwhelming majority at the State Duma, and political opposition is small and fragmented. Civil society is unable to exert any significant degree of control over government. Not surprisingly, the media now plays little part in exposing or criticising corruption.

The Kremlin's most recent measures, aimed at increasing the authorities' control over elections and the political process, prevent political parties from joining together to form coalitions. Regional governors are no longer elected, but appointed by the president.

A new law on non-governmental organizations, which came into force in April 2006, has been widely seen as a crackdown on human rights groups. St. Petersburg civil society campaigner Yury Vdovin called the law a weapon with a telescopic sight, to be used selectively against the most critical groups. Vdovin said that, through a new registration process, it will place major bureaucratic obstacles in the way of the work and possibly the existence of human rights groups. The law also restricts foreign funding for these groups.

"For friends—everything. For enemies—the law." This formula, invented by General Franco, provides a key to understanding Russia's current anti-corruption strategy.

In July 2006, the General Prosecutor's Office announced that corruption charges were being brought against two governors, Alexei Barinov of the Nenets Autonomous Region and Alexei Lebed of the Khakassia Republic.

The prosecutors maintain that Lebed twice travelled abroad at the expense of two local universities and Barinov misused hundreds of thousands of dollars of state money. On the surface, these cases look like good examples of an anti-corruption campaign in action.

But with investigations still in progress, there are some disturbing aspects. Both regions boast substantial oil and gas resources. And both governors have recently tried to assert their independence.

On May 14, Sergei Mironov, speaker of the Council of Federation called for the dismissal of four legislators on the grounds of allegations that they were they were involved in outside commercial deals. Two of the deputies represented Nenets Region and Khakassia, and Barinov and Lebed resisted the pressure from the Kremlin to support of sacking the MPs.

Justice in Russia is highly selective. As one democrat

politician puts it, "In Russia the law is used like a club. The law should be equal for everyone, while a club is used only against a chosen target."

The oil magnate, Mikhail Khodorkovsky, had the misfortune of becoming one such chosen target. His former company, Yukos, was declared bankrupt in July 2006 after being hit by a huge claim from the tax authorities for 734 billion rubles (US$27.5 billion). Khodorkovsky was sentenced in 2005 to eight years in prison for fraud and tax evasion.

Many believe he brought the disaster onto himself by breaking Putin's unwritten rule of politics, that oligarchs maybe be super-rich and influential as long as they don't mess with politics. Khodorkovsky, possibly with presidential ambitions, had openly funded political opposition and a critical TV channel.

One of Khodorkovsky's lawyers claimed that Saddam Hussein was being treated more fairly than his client.

"When Saddam's lawyers asked for an additional three months for him to familiarize himself with the case materials, they got a month and a half, but Khodorkovsky wasn't granted a single hour of the eight weeks he requested," said the lawyer, Yury Schmidt. "Instead of being sent to a prison in Moscow or in a neighboring region, Khodorkovsky was sent to a jail that is 7,000 km away from Moscow, which you can only reach by a six-hour flight and another half-day drive by car along a bumpy road."

In the world of media, pressure on journalists and attempted bribery is commonplace. One editor in St. Petersburg uses a trick to signal to readers when the contents of an

RUSSIA

article have been paid for by City Hall

He gives such articles a fictitious by-line, perhaps an anagram of the name of St. Petersburg governor Valentina Matvienko, or a name containing a reference to Smolny, the headquarters of the St. Petersburg City Hall.

An aide to an opposition parliamentarian in one Russian town admitted having a monthly "media allowance budget" that regularly buys his boss a quote, an interview or a feature in the local print media. The deputy has to pay to let readers know about his criticisms of the city government, but in this case the bribe is, ironically, helping one limited aspect of the democratic process to work.

For an alternative perspective, read the critical peer review commentary on this notebook, part of the 2006 Global Integrity Report (www.globalintegrity.org).

Senegal:
How to Make Money

By Hamadou Tidiane Sy

There's a French saying that "a boom in the building sector generates a boom for every other business." Now that Senegal is seeing a real construction boom, one would expect everything to boom as well—including corruption.

Many Senegalese will tell you there's no better place to make money (I have a friend who always differentiates between making money and earning money) than the construction and public works sector.

In Dakar in 2006, one can see the evidence on every corner: New buildings rise, roads are built and projects are launched almost every week. Yet people are becoming too rich too quickly in this poor African country, especially considering the low official incomes of civil servants and government officials.

The dilemma for anyone fighting for political integrity, stronger ethics and increased transparency is knowing how to progress from changing simple perceptions and beliefs, to the much more delicate and challenging task of proving corruption and bad governance, whether they are a journalist, academic or a member of civil society.

The construction sector is a perfect example of these challenges. Between July 2005 and June 2006, this industry became the stage of many corruption scandals, including the biggest scandal in Senegal's history since its independence in 1960.

It began when President Abdoulaye Wade accused his former Prime Minister Idrissa Seck of corruption in July 2005. Seck was swiftly investigated and sent to prison for embezzling public funds designated for reconstructing his hometown of Thiès. He was eventually released under circumstances that remain as unclear as the destination of the millions he allegedly stole, prompting his defenders to say that his case was simply "politically motivated."

In June 2006, an unknown young man named Malick Ndiaye accused Abdoulaye Baldé, a top civil servant in the office of the president, of allegedly receiving large bribes from private building companies involved in a huge public works project for renovating Dakar. Ndiaye was eventually taken to prison for defamation, but no serious investigation of Balde was undertaken, despite heavy media attention. The two examples help illustrate the different treatment garnered by "politically motivated" cases such as that of the former prime minister and "media generated" cases like that of Baldé.

The major obstacles to fighting corruption fall into three realms: institutional, political and social, according to Jacques Habib Sy, head of the Dakar-based non-governmental organization, Aid Transparency. "At the government level, there's a culture of secrecy inherited from the colonial times... and with it a marked tendency to classify every administrative document as a 'state secret,'" Sy said. This tendency makes access to information so difficult—even illegal—that anyone trying to expose corruption cases with documented evidence is easily caught in their own trap.

Mouhamadou Mbodj, coordinator of the anti-corruption watchdog Forum Civil, put it this way: "When you expose a corruption case as a journalist, you are accused of defaming someone and asked to bring the evidence you have. When you exhibit your evidence, you are accused of receiving and exposing administrative documents, which is equally punished by the law."

Three journalists working for the privately owned newspapers L'Observateur and le Courrier du Jour experienced this harsh legal reality when they decided to run a story then widely circulating in private circles alleging that Karim Wade, the son of the Senegalese president and one of his top advisers and confidantes, was involved in an illegal transfer of funds out of the country. In its December 2005 verdict, the court imposed heavy fines on all three journalists. Several other journalists and at least one opposition leader faced similar charges in 2005 and 2006. Journalists and civil society groups are becoming more frustrated with

SENEGAL

The Global Integrity Index:
How effective are Senegal's anti-corruption safeguards?

OVERALL RATING

Weak (65)

CATEGORY RATINGS

1) Civil Society, Public Information & Media — Very Weak (59)

2) Elections — Weak (62)

3) Government Accountability — Very Weak (50)

4) Administration & Civil Service — Very Weak (57)

5) Oversight & Regulation — Moderate (80)

6) Anti-Corruption & Rule of Law — Moderate (80)

(Scores range from 0 to 100)

The Global Integrity Index, through the Integrity Indicators, assesses the existence and effectiveness of national anti-corruption mechanisms. It does not measure corruption itself (which is nearly impossible). Instead, the Index analyzes the opposite of corruption: the institutions and practices that promote more accountable government and prevent, deter or punish corruption.

The Index is based on nearly 300 Integrity Indicators, discrete scores assigned by local experts using a consistent methodology and scoring criteria for each country. These results are then blindly peer reviewed at the local and international level to ensure consistency and accuracy.

All of the more than 11,000 Integrity Indicator scores that comprise the 2006 Index are published—along with extensive commentary, references and critical peer review comments and perspectives—in the annual Global Integrity Report.

For full results and downloadable datasets, see the Global Integrity website (www.globalintegrity.org).

the courts which, instead of asking alleged fraudsters to prove the origin of their wealth, are taking a tougher stance against whoever exposes misconduct. Whistle-blowers are encouraged in other countries and often afforded legal protection from the state.

Under these circumstances, one wonders how Senegal will achieve transparency and integrity in its public affairs. The government established the National Commission against Corruption and for Transparency in 2004, but its own members complain they do not have the legal or financial means to achieve substantial results. Furthermore, the Commission cannot take matters to court and only reports to the Senegalese president once a year.

Beyond these institutional and political hurdles, one must also face the more entrenched social and political realities of the country, where petty bribery and minor corruption are subtly veiled behind traditional social practices. Corruption spreads further in Senegalese society every day because "at the cultural level, there's a tacit acceptance of corrupt practices, which are perceived as a necessary step to accessing simple political, economic and social rights," Sy explained. In a society where gifts are socially accepted, it is difficult to differentiate between a "genuine" gift and one given by a political leader or wealthy businessman to anyone who may expose him or witness his shady deeds.

Because of these social and cultural values, "tackling petty corruption may be difficult," said Pape Samba Kane, a journalist who recently published a book revealing how

SENEGAL

business leaders and other people in power manipulate Senegal's laws. However, he said, "it is no excuse. State corruption is vulnerable when people start combating it through scientifically proven methods."

For an alternative perspective, read the critical peer review commentary on this notebook, part of the 2006 Global Integrity Report (www.globalintegrity.org).

Serbia:
Sort of Like Taxes

By Miomir Brkic

"I don't want a bottle of scotch, I'm not an alcoholic. I just need the money to pay for my expenses at the doctors' conference in the U.K." This is how a Serbian doctor from Belgrade refused a gift of scotch from a patient he successfully treated: He expected money for services rendered.

He is only one of many doctors who demand bribes, which are seen by Serbian citizens as an unavoidable step in a corrupt medical system. Though the government has asked citizens not to pay bribes and to report doctors who demand them, the practice has not abated. Serbians coming to the country's capital for medical treatment—particularly those from rural areas—always budget extra money to pay for a hospital bed or some extra attention from their doctor, which can cost 6,549 dinars (US$100) and up depending on the type of service.

Judges are no better. When Serbian justice minister

Zoran Stojkovic said in July 2006 that the level of corruption had significantly increased, he was just the latest official to publicly acknowledge what every citizen realizes—that criminals can buy their freedom. Police have arrested judges and prosecutors, including a supreme court judge and the deputy state prosecutor, for taking hundreds of thousands of dollars in bribes in exchange for acquitting members of criminal gangs.

In many regions, the practice persists of paying for services from municipal administrators with a pound of coffee or a box of candy. This type of corruption is hard to uproot, particularly when authorities show little interest in tackling it, and citizens perceive it as a sort of tax.

Serbians are more aware of corruption in state institutions. According to a survey published in mid-2006 by Transparency International Serbia (TI Serbia—*Transparentnost Srbija*) and the Westminster Foundation for Democracy, nearly 40 percent of citizens think corruption is highest in the judiciary system, while 25 to 30 percent believe corruption exists in local and central governments, as well as the police and the media.

Most Serbians also believe that systemic corruption in higher levels of government is more dangerous than petty corruption. Large scale interference with state functions and the weaknesses of independent oversight institutions underlie several scandals involving government administration officials.

Commenting on a World Bank report that called corruption widespread in Serbia, Verica Barac, chairwoman of the Anti-Corruption Council, blamed the government and parliament. Though the Council is a government advisory body established by Zoran Djindjic, the first democratically elected prime minister of Serbia, the current government responded to Barac with complete indifference. In contrast, TI Serbia said the World Bank report, which called on the administration to "demonstrate considerably more political will for the crackdown on corruption," was a cause for significant concern.

So far, the government's performance in the fight against corruption has not been impressive. Authorities have enacted an anti-corruption strategy, passed several anti-corruption laws in areas such as public procurement and funding for political parties, and established a number of regulatory bodies in telecommunications, broadcasting and other industries. Unfortunately these regulatory bodies are largely decorative, many of them launched as purely political moves. After visiting Serbia, Alistair Graham, Chairman of the U.K. Committee on Standards in Public Life, said Serbia has taken the wrong approach to fighting corruption: Authorities are obsessed with laws, while public institutions lack codes of conduct and are filled with bad examples of corrupt officials.

Government officials are inclined to intervene in state functions, frequently trying to manage economic processes and act as arbiters in the market. For example, the minister of capital investment participated directly in the procurement of used train engines and cars for the state railway company. The deal was closed without a cost schedule or the public tender required by law. When funds went unaccounted for, the minister himself closed the case, stating he ordered a

SERBIA

The Global Integrity Index:
How effective are Serbia's
anti-corruption safeguards?

OVERALL RATING
Weak (64)

CATEGORY RATINGS
1) Civil Society, Public Information & Media — Strong (81)

2) Elections — Moderate (74)

3) Government Accountability — Very Weak (53)

4) Administration & Civil Service — Very Weak (30)

5) Oversight & Regulation — Weak (69)

6) Anti-Corruption & Rule of Law — Moderate (78)

(Scores range from 0 to 100)

The Global Integrity Index, through the Integrity Indicators, assesses the existence and effectiveness of national anti-corruption mechanisms. It does not measure corruption itself (which is nearly impossible). Instead, the Index analyzes the opposite of corruption: the institutions and practices that promote more accountable government and prevent, deter or punish corruption.

The Index is based on nearly 300 Integrity Indicators, discrete scores assigned by local experts using a consistent methodology and scoring criteria for each country. These results are then blindly peer reviewed at the local and international level to ensure consistency and accuracy.

All of the more than 11,000 Integrity Indicator scores that comprise the 2006 Index are published—along with extensive commentary, references and critical peer review comments and perspectives—in the annual Global Integrity Report.

For full results and downloadable datasets, see the Global Integrity website (www.globalintegrity.org).

police investigation that found no evidence of embezzlement.

Months later, the defense minister and several of his officers were accused of accepting bribes from a local military equipment supplier with whom the minister cut a deal, also without a public tender. The same minister was sacked for his involvement in a spy-satellite rental scandal, though legal proceedings are ongoing.

Though the Anti-Corruption Council composed a report several thousand pages long documenting the involvement of the former central bank governor and current finance minister in a case involving the sale of the National Savings Bank, the minister denied the charges and the government did nothing.

The business community was shocked at the government's interference in the case of a mineral water manufacturer in which the government illegally took the role of arbiter in the proprietary documents market from the Securities Commission. To support its candidate in the sale, the government, in a late-night session, ordered prosecutors to threaten the Securities Commission with arrest.

After adopting a national strategy, the government suggested abolishing the Anti-Corruption Council and forming a new anti-corruption agency. However, some worry such an agency would become just another bureaucratic apparatus under government control, itself susceptible to corruption. The government has refused to propose a law to parliament establishing an independent ombudsman to mediate corruption complaints.

The government's unwillingness to subject itself

SERBIA

to oversight has proven an essential problem in fighting corruption. An important example involves the law on access to information. An independent trustee appointed to implement the law has asked the government almost once a month for the last year to allow access to information of public significance. So far, the government has not responded to his requests.

The biggest potential beneficiaries of the law are the media, which could also play an important role in government oversight. However, the media's engagement has so far been reduced to sensationalist coverage lacking analysis or investigative approaches. This is probably because most of the media is under indirect control of the ruling parties and the businessmen who finance them.

Many nongovernmental organizations have conducted surveys on the cause of corruption and credible measures of suppressing it. At this point, however, the government does not seem to understand that all segments of society must be included in such an effort—including the government itself.

For an alternative perspective, read the critical peer review commentary on this notebook, part of the 2006 Global Integrity Report (www.globalintegrity.org).

Sierra Leone:
Integrity is the Exception
By Charlie Hughes

One evening in June 2006, a friend and I talked over drinks with two women who had just finished their exams at the University of Sierra Leone. We spoke about exams, good and bad lecturers, and cheating. I asked the students whether it was possible to bribe their lecturers for better grades. The women swore they have not heard of this at their college. But they could not be sure.

Corruption is pervasive in Sierra Leone, so there is always this doubt. Integrity is the exception, not the rule.

I myself am culpable. When it was time to renew my car's annual license this year, I didn't bother to go the licensing authority. I gave 297,483 leones (US$100) to a friend of mine who passed it onto somebody who worked at the licensing authority.

I had been complaining to my friend that I was too busy and didn't have time to go and renew my license. My friend told me that he knew somebody at the licensing office who could do it for me. It would have cost me about 208,238 leones (US$70) to license my four-wheel drive car. I paid 297,483 leones (US$100) to spare myself the hassle. In the evening my friend came by with the license.

The vehicle licensing authority is by no means alone in this behavior. Everything is for sale. One can even buy a death or birth certificate at the Births and Deaths Office for a fictitious death or birth!

You can register a company at the Registrar General's office in 48 hours for a bulk fee paid to a senior official there. The bulk fee would include charges payable to government and extras for the official doing the legwork. You can skip the extra payments to any official but your company will not been registered in less than three weeks. When registering a company, you are required to first submit its name to ascertain whether any other company carries the same name. A clerk manually searches the names. The search will last for weeks if the clerk's palms are not greased. Of course, the clerk behaves as if he has the ability to determine the pace at which he can confirm your company's name.

I cited earlier the possibility of licensing a vehicle without it being physically inspected, or acquiring certificates for fictitious births and deaths. Corruption in these instances is about the willingness to bribe public officials when we fall short of procedural requirements, seek to beat bureaucratic processes or to ask public officials to ignore petty wrong doings.

Bribes enable citizens to shorten or bypass procedures with public officials. We easily use money to "shake hands" with public officials. It is commonly accepted—a way to say "thanks" for the job the official does.

Of course, public officials must willingly accept the bribes to complete the corrupt transaction. And maybe the habit persists because there is always a look on public officials' faces that seems to ask, "What's in this for me?" Many times, that question is even asked directly.

In fact, petty corruption is largely based around public officials' infusion of this question into public service. People's decisions to "shake hands" with a bribe are often skillfully prompted by the discretion public officials hold in these transactions.

This manipulation of discretion permeates every level of the public service. Senior officers determine when to sign your papers when you apply for state land, a telephone line, passport or mining license. Secretaries have the choice to give or not to give you application forms or book an appointment for you to see the Permanent Secretary.

Information about how one could go about securing a public service is also a discretionary transaction. That is why at the Customs Department there are lots of people hanging around "volunteering" for a fee to help you navigate procedures to clear your goods.

I should make the point, however, that these transactions do not have to work this way. The environment exists for members of the public to demand and get clean public services, or be involved in tackling corruption.

The ombudsman, for instance, says that a good number of complaints from individuals that his office has settled

The Global Integrity Index:
How effective are Sierra Leone's
anti-corruption safeguards?

OVERALL RATING

Very Weak (56)

CATEGORY RATINGS

1) Civil Society, Public Information & Media — Very Weak (51)

2) Elections — Weak (61)

3) Government Accountability — Very Weak (46)

4) Administration & Civil Service — Very Weak (55)

5) Oversight & Regulation — Very Weak (57)

6) Anti-Corruption & Rule of Law — Weak (68)

(Scores range from 0 to 100)

The Global Integrity Index, through the Integrity Indicators,
assesses the existence and effectiveness of national anti-corruption
mechanisms. It does not measure corruption itself (which is nearly
impossible). Instead, the Index analyzes the opposite of corruption: the institutions and practices that promote more accountable
government and prevent, deter or punish corruption.

The Index is based on nearly 300 Integrity Indicators, discrete
scores assigned by local experts using a consistent methodology and
scoring criteria for each country. These results are then blindly peer
reviewed at the local and international level to ensure consistency
and accuracy.

All of the more than 11,000 Integrity Indicator scores that
comprise the 2006 Index are published—along with extensive commentary, references and critical peer review comments and perspectives—in the annual Global Integrity Report.

For full results and downloadable datasets, see the Global
Integrity website (www.globalintegrity.org).

relate to public officials refusing or unnecessarily wasting time to provide public service.

There are District Budget Oversight Committees comprised of ordinary citizens established by the Ministry of Finance in all 12 administrative districts in the country. District Budget Oversight Committees monitor the implementation of public services and contracts awarded from public funds and report discrepancies to the Ministry of Finance or Anti-Corruption Commission. Indeed, reports by District Budget Oversight Committees have in some cases led to investigations by the police or the Anti-Corruption Commission.

Civil society organizations have ventured into the widening space for citizens' involvement in tackling corruption. Among the most prominent is the Network Movement for Justice and Development (NMJD). NMJD has been monitoring the implementation of contracts awarded by the government from the Highly Indebted Poor Country Initiative funds provided by international donors. In May 2006 the organization released a damning report detailing projects that were not completed, badly done, or totally abandoned.

In August 2005 the chairman of the Town Council of Makeni, the regional capitol of the Northern province resigned from office. The resignation was the culmination of a battle waged by local civil society organizations for months against the chairman on allegations that he misappropriated tens of thousands of U.S. dollars.

The government has made its own claims about the progress of processes like the Public Expenditure Tracking

SIERRA LEONE

Survey (PETS) and institutions like the Anti-Corruption Commission. Since 2001 a PETS has been annually undertaken by the Ministry of Finance to track the effective and intended utilization of public service delivery funds allocated to ministries, departments and agencies. The PETS in 2002-2003 exposed that 50 percent of government school fee subsidies were lost to corruption. The government acted on this and is now able to claim that today 90 percent of school fee subsidies reach their intended beneficiaries.

Who in the big towns and cities has not heard the Anti-Corruption Commission's slogan on the radio in our native tongue: *"de yie day wach!"* The eye is watching!

We are still talking about the on-going trial of a former minister of transport and communication, a former chairman of the Sierra Leone Ports Authority, a former accountant general and a former permanent secretary in the Ministry of Transport and Communication. The four officials were charged in a fraud scandal in May 2005 over a 791 million leone (US$266,000) transaction to buy a forklift for the Sierra Leone Ports Authority.

And in Freetown, who has not heard the name Gloria Newman-Smart? After less than two years as chief immigration officer, the late Newman-Smart was accused selling 26 illegal passports for 1.5 million leones (US$520). The Anti-Corruption Commission investigated and determined that although no offense under the Anti-Corruption Act could be proved, there was a clear breach of procedure.

On January 19, 2006 a magistrate was convicted on a four-count charge of soliciting a bribe, in a prosecution by

the Anti-Corruption Commission. A senior official of the
ruling Sierra Leone People's Party insists that with instances
like these, the threat that the "eye is watching" cannot be
taken lightly.

The media, civil society organizations and opposition
parties see it a little bit differently. They say the Anti-
Corruption Commission is nowhere near its best, citing the
government's unwillingness to prosecute certain cases. A case
that is often cited is that of Okere Adams, former minister
of marine resources, who is now minister of tourism. In
2005, the Anti-Corruption Commission arrested Adams on
corruption allegations involving donor funds. However, the
investigation remains stalled and to this day the matter has
not found its way into the courts.

Corruption is the most talked about governance
challenge facing the country. It is debated in taxis, at pubs
and work places. Every day newspapers in the country run
stories about fraud or the misappropriation of public funds
by government officials and businessmen. Commentaries and
editorials on the pervasiveness of corruption abound in the
media. Local songs like *"Borboh Belleh,"* about the ills and
pervasiveness of corruption were hits last year.

But it is interesting to note that people hardly talk about
the little bribes they pay to public officials.

The international community has fueled the corruption
debate in Sierra Leone. In May 2005, United Nations Secretary
General Kofi Annan issued a report on Seirra Leone to the
United Nations Security Council. In that report, Annan
said that citizens could see little progress in the fight against

SIERRA LEONE

corruption. The government vehemently disputed the report.

One cannot help but reflect on the intensity of the corruption debate in relation to the number of anti-corruption institutions and processes that currently operate in the country. Are our hearts soothed when the Anti-Corruption Commission lists the tens of corruption cases it has initiated? Do we wail or hail when the citizens' organization NMJD reports that hundred of millions of leones of debt relief funds are lost through abandoned or never completed contracts?

In the fight against corruption, the message is mixed. Can I choose to see the glass as half full?

The head of state suggested as much in a speech to Parliament on June 23, 2006. President Kabbah said that the days when corruption could not be discussed were over. "Rather than being tolerated or exalted, reports of corrupt practices anywhere, particularly in government, are now regarded with the greatest contempt and, where proven, those involved attract lawful punishment and scorn in the society."

He paints an encouraging picture. On the contrary, opposition politicians that I spoke to in preparing this report were unanimous in their view: they see a glass that is very nearly empty.

For an alternative perspective, read the critical peer review commentary on this notebook, part of the 2006 Global Integrity Report (www.globalintegrity.org).

Sudan:
Seeds of Disaster
By Alfred Taban Logune

Sudan is commonly considered among the world's most corrupt countries, yet this is very difficult to prove due to a secretive government and years of strict media controls, which have all but eliminated journalists' watchdog abilities.

President Lt. Gen. Omar Hassan al-Bashir came to power in June 1989, toppling the democratically elected government of Prime Minister al-Sadiq al-Mahdi. The new government claimed it wanted to rid Sudan of corruption, financial mismanagement, nepotism and the military failures in South Sudan. However, within a short time, it had shut down all independent newspapers, jailed dozens of journalists and writers, dissolved Parliament and trade unions and banned all political parties. Real and perceived opponents of the new Islamic-oriented government were thrown into prison and many of their businesses were taken over by members of the government or their affiliates.

A new paramilitary group known as the Popular

Defence Force (PDF) launched a military offensive to wipe out the rebel Sudan People's Liberation Army (SPLA) in the south of the country. In the 1990s, vast wealth was added to the equation when oil production began in the Unity state in South Sudan. Around the same time, a widespread campaign of torching homes and villages began to displace residents.

There were virtually no independent organizations to question the government. The seeds of corruption and lack of transparency were planted.

Bidding for government contracts, particularly in the oil sector, is still not public and contracts are awarded to people close to the regime. In one such case, a contractor charged with supplying fish to the PDF in Jebel Aulia, a suburb of Khartoum, enriched himself very quickly. The amounts he charged for his deliveries were rarely questioned, according to a Southern Sudanese lawyer who knows the individual.

People close to the government hurriedly set up companies, many in Malaysia and China, to take advantage of the newfound oil money, as did the ruling National Congress Party. One such company—based in China and owned by the National Congress—reportedly skims a commission of 35 percent for all trade with Sudan. Bilateral trade between Sudan and China has been valued at 249 billion dinars (US$1.2 billion) a year in recent years, although last year it dropped to around 177 billon dinars (US$850 million), according to official figures.

But not all of Sudan's corruption is on such a grand scale. In August 2006, James Henry Tadiwe, the minister of rural development and infrastructure in the West Bahr al-

Ghazal state in South Sudan was suspended on the grounds that he embezzled 14 million dinars (US$67,000) allocated for drilling boreholes in the state.

SPLA separatists also are engaged in corruption. Military commanders sell off timber and other resources in the south and pocket the profits.

Taxes in Sudan are so high that business owners post fictitious profits to avoid them. Companies pay a 5-percent stamp duty tax, a 10-percent value-added tax and a business profit tax, as well as 18 percent of employee salaries for social insurance.

Sudan's chaotic liberalization and currency changeover in 1992 led to widespread corruption. The liberalization of the economy, introduced by the government, attracted both local and foreign investment. As a result both struggling and profitable corporations were sold off for virtually nothing. One example is the Grand Hotel in Khartoum, which was sold to a Malaysian firm. Large sums of money went to individuals, while very little entered the Treasury. And when the country's currency was changed from Sudanese pounds to Sudanese dinars during a two-week period, millions of latecomers lost most of their money.

On Jan. 9, 2005, the government in Khartoum and the rebel Sudan Peoples' Liberation Movement signed the Comprehensive Peace Agreement (CPA). According to the agreement, the two parties are expected to share equally the oil proceeds found in South Sudan. The majority of Sudan's oil is in South Sudan, but Khartoum may keep all revenue from oil pumped elsewhere in the country. Early in 2006, the

SUDAN

The Global Integrity Index:
How effective are Sudan's anti-corruption safeguards?

OVERALL RATING

Very Weak (59)

CATEGORY RATINGS

1) Civil Society, Public Information & Media — Very Weak (58)

2) Elections — Very Weak (53)

3) Government Accountability — Weak (62)

4) Administration & Civil Service — Very Weak (57)

5) Oversight & Regulation — Weak (65)

6) Anti-Corruption & Rule of Law — Very Weak (60)

(Scores range from 0 to 100)

The Global Integrity Index, through the Integrity Indicators, assesses the existence and effectiveness of national anti-corruption mechanisms. It does not measure corruption itself (which is nearly impossible). Instead, the Index analyzes the opposite of corruption: the institutions and practices that promote more accountable government and prevent, deter or punish corruption.

The Index is based on nearly 300 Integrity Indicators, discrete scores assigned by local experts using a consistent methodology and scoring criteria for each country. These results are then blindly peer reviewed at the local and international level to ensure consistency and accuracy.

All of the more than 11,000 Integrity Indicator scores that comprise the 2006 Index are published—along with extensive commentary, references and critical peer review comments and perspectives—in the annual Global Integrity Report.

For full results and downloadable datasets, see the Global Integrity website (www.globalintegrity.org).

government of South Sudan said it had received about US$750 million in about a year after the CPA was signed. However the President of South Sudan, Salva Kiir, complained that his government was not sure whether it was getting its fair share of the oil wealth, as called for in the CPA.

Kiir was quoted in the Khartoum Monitor newspaper as saying that the border between north and south has not been stationery and that his government was not sure where the oil was being pumped. Kiir also said in newspaper interviews in July that the petroleum commission charged with monitoring whether the South was receiving its fair share of oil revenue had not been functioning. The disagreement between the National Congress Party and South Sudan's government centered on who would head the Ministry of Energy and Mining. The government of South Sudan fought in September 2005 to choose the minister, but ultimately, Awad al-Jaz, a National Congress member, was appointed to the post.

Much of Sudan's budget is allocated to military spending. Although fighting in South Sudan stopped after the signing of the CPA, fighting has been going on since February 2003 in Darfur in western Sudan. [At press time, conflict in Sudan is increasing.] Military budgets are not disclosed and the government selects defense contractors secretly in the name of national security. Disclosing military secrets is a capital offense. Supplies to the Army and the PDF are channelled through companies and individuals close to the government. The Army is reported to be spending one million dollars a day, according to unofficial sources. There has been little transparency: Information usually comes from individuals

SUDAN

in the government who want to see changes toward more openness or those close to, but not part of, the regime.

Although the government has said it does not tolerate corruption, only a few bank employees who have embezzled funds have been arrested and prosecuted. Unofficially, only two senior government officials have been fired on corruption charges, and they have not been prosecuted. One was a state governor who was accused in the early 1990s of using public funds to furnish his private house. The other was Col. Martin Malwal, a former member of Bashir's 15-man junta that overthrew al-Mahdi's government. In 1994, Malwal was removed for allegedly taking public funds to buy flats in neighboring Egypt. Malwal was later reinstated to the Council of Ministers.

Instead of reining in corruption, the government has cracked down on the press for writing about it. The Arabic daily Alternative View (*al-Rai al-Akhier*) was closed down in 2002 when it accused a government official, Mahjoub al-Khalifa, now a presidential advisor, of embezzling millions of dollars meant for providing services in the Khartoum state. In 2003, the privately owned Nation (*Al Watan*) Arabic daily was shut down and its editor, Sid Ahmed Khalifa, detained when it reported on the corrupt practices surrounding Vice President Ali Osman Mohamed Taha.

The Islamic banking system in Sudan, under which interest charges are forbidden, also enables much corruption. Banks become participants in the businesses they help begin. When the businesses make money, it is shared according to the capital each creditor has invested; when there is a loss, it also is shared. Many banks have lost millions of Sudanese pounds due to unscrupulous clients.

Despite clear provisions in the 2005 CPA and a May 2006 Darfur treaty for press freedoms and open and clean government, wars and once-strict government controls on media have allowed corruption in Sudan to flourish. Although the media restrictions have been relaxed, few reporters have dared to dig deep into cases of government corruption.

For an alternative perspective, read the critical peer review commentary on this notebook, part of the 2006 Global Integrity Report (www.globalintegrity.org).

SUDAN

Tajikistan:
How to Frighten Investors
By Nargis Zokirova

Corruption in Tajikistan has gone beyond the social level, reaching the political and economic strata. The whole system of executive power is penetrated by corruption, inhibiting the developing economy of Tajikistan.

Bribing is a normal habit in every sector of the governmental departments of Tajikistan. Tajiks are used to giving bribes for everything: to get jobs, enroll in universities and pass exams, to get driver's licenses, to pay taxes, to get passports and so on. That is why Tajikistan was ranked by Transparency International as one of the most corrupt countries in the world.

According to Khodjimuhammad Umarov, an independent economist, the majority of the Tajik population takes part in corrupt practices. The 2005 report "Corruption in Tajikistan: Public Opinion" was provided by the Tajik president's Strategic Research Center, the Swiss Agency for Development and Cooperation and the United Nations

Development Program. According to this report, ordinary people bribe officials up to three times a year.

Businessmen and entrepreneurs are more prone to giving bribes than any other part of the population. For them, giving bribes is a daily reality. Likewise, anybody who wants to start a business becomes a victim of the corrupt system. The officials also must pay for services or render services in order to see their problems solved. It was said that 34 percent of officials confirmed having paid bribes or rendering services to "necessary people" over the last three years.

Abdulvokhid Shamolov, the head of a task group, claimed that "corruption in Tajikistan leads to political discredit of the state authority." Legal institutions, judicial authority, health and education authorities, tax and custom services, trade and transport are all polluted by internal corruption. Bribery (65 percent), nepotism (25 percent), subornation of officials (15 percent), machinations with the state property (10 percent), blackmail from officials (15 percent) and bribery of university teachers and physicians (30 percent) are the most prevalent types of corruption in Tajikistan, according to the above-mentioned report. By respondents' opinions, bribery as a main type of corruption is narrowly connected with nepotism and machinations with the state property.

Over the last six months, Tajik mass media have revealed 120 corruption crimes, which were then referred to Abdurasul Kholmurodov, the head of the Anti-Corruption Department of the D.A.'s office. Sixty-five criminal cases involving 82 Tajik citizens were opened. The loss to the state

TAJIKISTAN

The Global Integrity Index:
How effective are Tajikistan's
anti-corruption safeguards?

OVERALL RATING

Very Weak (50)

CATEGORY RATINGS

1) Civil Society, Public Information & Media — Very Weak (59)

2) Elections — Very Weak (55)

3) Government Accountability — Very Weak (17)

4) Administration & Civil Service — Very Weak (53)

5) Oversight & Regulation — Very Weak (46)

6) Anti-Corruption & Rule of Law — Moderate (71)

(Scores range from 0 to 100)

The Global Integrity Index, through the Integrity Indicators, assesses the existence and effectiveness of national anti-corruption mechanisms. It does not measure corruption itself (which is nearly impossible). Instead, the Index analyzes the opposite of corruption: the institutions and practices that promote more accountable government and prevent, deter or punish corruption.

The Index is based on nearly 300 Integrity Indicators, discrete scores assigned by local experts using a consistent methodology and scoring criteria for each country. These results are then blindly peer reviewed at the local and international level to ensure consistency and accuracy.

All of the more than 11,000 Integrity Indicator scores that comprise the 2006 Index are published—along with extensive commentary, references and critical peer review comments and perspectives—in the annual Global Integrity Report.

For full results and downloadable datasets, see the Global Integrity website (www.globalintegrity.org).

budget was US$134,000. Kholmurodov said that the quantity of identified crimes increased many times in comparison with the previous year. The largest number of corruption cases was in health and education.

Umarov, the economist who studies corruption, noted that the struggle against corruption takes place only in schools, universities and hospitals in Tajikistan. The entrenched high-level officials, with access to large sums from the state treasury available for payoffs, remain above the law. "This is clear," Umarov said. "The high-level official holds power and has money. He can bribe any investigator. In the case of teachers, they have to take bribes because it is very difficult to manage with (US)$30 to (US)$40 a month."

Mahmadali Vatanov, first deputy of the Supreme Court, said judges on the Tajik Supreme Court earned an average of US$300 a month, while lower-level judges earn up to US$150 a month. Meanwhile, a minimal monthly wage is about US$7.50. Despite their high salaries, some judges have been found taking bribes. One corrupt judge recently was brought to justice, receiving a sentence of five years in prison.

Some experts say the high level of corruption in Tajikistan discourages foreign investment, a problem also recognized by Tajik authorities. They are aware that Tajikistan, with external debts of US$828 million, cannot manage without foreign investment.

"Investors are sure to succeed, if equal conditions are available to them," said Richard Hoagland, U.S. ambassador to Tajikistan from 2003 to August 2006, speaking at a meeting with journalists in July 2006. "Transparency and law enforcement give confidence to the American investors, but corruption and official circumlocution can frighten them away," Hoagland added.

Tajikistan has a good chance of becoming a member of the World Trade Organization (WTO) during the coming two to three years, said Sobir Kurbanov of the Swiss Agency for Development and Cooperation's office in Tajikistan. He said that to join the WTO, Tajikistan will need to fight corruption, observe and fulfill the laws of foreign commerce and have stronger state management and better prepared specialists.

Abdulvohid Shamolov, head of the Strategic Research Center's "Corruption in Tajikistan: Public Opinion" report, said the converse also is true: that any further rise of corruption can lead the country to political and economic isolation, complicating its internal political situation.

Muso Asozoda, the head of personnel of the National Democratic Party of Tajikistan, said corruption as a pernicious phenomenon takes place not only in Tajikistan, but in industrialized countries as well. According to Asozoda, the high level of corruption is linked with consequences of the Tajik Civil War, which took place between 1992 and 1997.

Shokirdjon Khakimov, first deputy of Social Democratic Party, said the most common form of corruption in Tajikistan is nepotism, especially among high-powered authorities. "A group of President (Emomali) Rahmonov's compatriots from the south still run us. They came to power in the beginning of the Civil War and still influence the condition and levels of corruption," Khakimov said.

That assessment is backed by a 2005 report by Brussels-based Crisis International Group, which stated that "the president surrounded himself with people originating from his region." One of the report's conclusions is that these people block the struggle against corruption in Tajikistan.

In Umarov's opinion, it is impossible to control corruption in the country. "I believe that the authorities are guilty of creating this kind of situation, because until recently the Tajik government denied the presence of corruption amongst officials," he said. "The amazing fact is that the first to speak about the existence of corruption in Tajikistan were the international organizations, which were not accredited here. After initially denying these facts, the Tajik officials had to finally acknowledge them and recognize the presence of corruption in the country."

However, Rahmonov himself pays special attention to fighting corruption, issuing several key legislative statements since 1999. Among them are "President's Decree about Additional Steps to Strengthen the Fight against Economic Crimes and Corruption," "Law about Fighting Corruption," and "Law about State Service." The president created the Office for Fighting Corruption in 2004 to extirpate this pernicious phenomenon.

Saifullo Safarov, head of the presidential Strategic Research Center, said the president has chosen a two-pronged approach to fight corruption: by accepting the new laws and by public opinion. "Repressive measures, which are common in many countries in their fight against corruption, do not give the expected results. This is the same as struggling with alcoholism," Safarov said. He believes that "freedom

TAJIKISTAN

of speech and independent mass media can effectively fight corruption. The development of these two institutions can lead to the increase of responsibility in all levels of society, from officials to common citizens."

For an alternative perspective, read the critical peer review commentary on this notebook, part of the 2006 Global Integrity Report (www.globalintegrity.org).

Tanzania:
The Ringing Cry

By Sebastian Sanga

There is a loud cry ringing out in every Tanzanian city:
the outcry over corruption in the Ministry of Land, Housing
and Human Settlement. Dubious deals have found their
lucrative place in this ministry: residential and commercial
houses on public open spaces, double allocation of plots and
the haphazard mushrooming of petrol stations, among other
violations. In a 2005 report, the Prevention of Corruption
Bureau (PCB) confirmed that corruption was deep-rooted
in the land sector, revealing, among other travesties, that
property appraisers collaborated with land officers to falsify
title deeds. Approving and issuing building permits is such
a slow process that citizens are compelled to pay bribes
for every stage, from typing the certificate to obtaining the
land commissioner's signature, often totaling some 135,000
shillings (US$105) on top of official fees.

President Benjamini Mkapa, whose administration
ended in November 2005, had vowed to adopt openness

and transparency, but failed to live up to his promise. Land Minister John Magufuli told Parliament in August 2006 that his officials were "dirty", and that some, including Deputy Minister Rita Mlaki, owned questionable plots for speculative purposes. Ms. Mlaki refutes the allegations, but the new president, Mr. Jakaya Kikwete, has admitted that the Land Ministry is one of the government's most corrupt.

Unfortunately, The Land Ministry is not the only one rendered immovable by the crippling disease of corruption. The Controller and Auditor General estimates that over 20 percent of the government's budget in each fiscal year is lost to corruption, including theft, fraud and fake purchasing transactions. The list of victims constitutes a litany of public woes.

The privatization process has seen numerous controversial orders flow from the top down. Members of Parliament (MPs) who represent the public interest seem overpowered by those with less integrity. Former Finance Minister Basil Pesambili Mramba, who currently serves as minister of infrastructure development, wrote a controversial letter in September 2005 extending the port of Dar es Salaam's container terminal lease contract from 10 to 25 years without following proper procedures.

The letter, marked confidential, informed Tanzania Revenue Authority Commissioner General Harry Kitillya about the extension of the lease agreement between the Parastatal Sector Reform Commission and Tanzania Container Terminal Services, a local partnership between a Philippines-based company and Vertex Financial Services of

Dar es Salaam, which earns more than 140 billion shillings (US$11 million) per month. Normally the PSRC would sign a lease after following required procedures including consultations with stakeholders.

Rampant corruption also has engulfed the procurement system, where billions of shillings sink into the wrong hands every year. In July 2006, the Ministry of Finance came up with a proposal to write off debts worth over 46 billion shillings (US$3.6 million). Skeptical MPs, especially from the opposition wing, wanted to form a committee to investigate why debtors had reneged on their commitments. One case singled out for scrutiny involved KJ Motors, which never delivered on a 147 million-shilling (US$115,000) contract to supply motor vehicles. The Parliamentary Public Accounts Committee said signs pointed to corrupt public servants and their liaisons with notoriously dirty businessmen.

While such graft keeps Tanzanians poor, corruption in the Ministry of Health and its agencies, such as the Tanzania Food and Drugs Agency (TFDA), actually puts their lives at risk. Counterfeit drugs abound in pharmacies as officials continue to solicit bribes from illegal dealers, and many of the HIV testing kits supplied to hospitals are defective. The contract that granted two companies exclusive rights to sell HIV rapid-test kits in Tanzania is shrouded in suspicion. Tanzania tested several HIV kits for national distribution a few years ago, but senior officials at the Ministry of Health and Social Welfare decided to include only the Capillus kit, manufactured by the Irish company Trinity Biotech and Determine HIV, manufactured the American firm Abbot

The Global Integrity Index:
How effective are Tanzania's anti-corruption safeguards?

OVERALL RATING
Very Weak (59)

CATEGORY RATINGS
1) Civil Society, Public Information & Media — Weak (63)

2) Elections — Very Weak (56)

3) Government Accountability — Very Weak (48)

4) Administration & Civil Service — Very Weak (55)

5) Oversight & Regulation — Weak (67)

6) Anti-Corruption & Rule of Law — Weak (66)

(Scores range from 0 to 100)

The Global Integrity Index, through the Integrity Indicators, assesses the existence and effectiveness of national anti-corruption mechanisms. It does not measure corruption itself (which is nearly impossible). Instead, the Index analyzes the opposite of corruption: the institutions and practices that promote more accountable government and prevent, deter or punish corruption.

The Index is based on nearly 300 Integrity Indicators, discrete scores assigned by local experts using a consistent methodology and scoring criteria for each country. These results are then blindly peer reviewed at the local and international level to ensure consistency and accuracy.

All of the more than 11,000 Integrity Indicator scores that comprise the 2006 Index are published—along with extensive commentary, references and critical peer review comments and perspectives—in the annual Global Integrity Report.

For full results and downloadable datasets, see the Global Integrity website (www.globalintegrity.org).

Laboratories. Both products, distributed solely by Bharat Rajan's Biocare Health Products Company, are now outdated as HIV rapid-test kits, as they detect the virus when antibodies develop after an attack, while the latest generation of test kits are able to detect it as soon as it enters a person's bloodstream by detecting antigens. Further, the Capillus kit had failed to meet key benchmarks set up by the ministry that tested the kits. The media, which reported widely on the story, linked the companies' monopoly on the test kits to corruption.

Unfortunately, the Tanzanian courts offer no recourse. In a 2005 public survey by the PCB, 97 percent of respondents said corruption was rampant in the country's judiciary. The study also tracked the various forms that corruption takes at different stages. At the beginning of the legal process, court clerks ask for bribes from people filing cases. Failure to pay may have devastating consequences, such as deliberately hidden or misplaced documents. At the hearing stage, corruption manifests as delays in setting hearings, vague or contradictory orders, improperly filed documents and deliberate omission to record court proceedings. And at the verdict stage, cases are dismissed on technical grounds or vague interpretation of the law and judgments are delayed. Factors such as poor remuneration, poor working facilities and inadequate supervision tempt judicial personnel to the dark side. Resident magistrates rarely make more than 100,000 shillings (US$80), without benefits. High court judges make over 500,000 shillings (US$390), supplemented with other fringe benefits.

Elections in Tanzania don't fare much better.

Corruption was especially rampant during the 2005 campaign, when the ruling Revolutionary State Party (CCM — *Chama Cha Mapinduzi*) reportedly distributed cash, mobile phones and other rewards to voters. The CCM is known for using election law provisions that allow candidates to offer hospitality, gifts, and favors—known as *takrima*—to constituents during campaigns. The law does not limit the form, amount or duration of such gifts, creating what critics call a "loophole for corruption"—particularly pernicious since the CCM received significantly greater government subsidies under the law than other parties. The High Court recently banned *takrima*.

Former CCM Secretary General Philip Mangula criticized the PCB for failing to curb corruption in the electoral process. Tanzania's anti-corruption laws are governed by the Prevention of Corruption Act, a poorly designed law. The PCB has sections, which make the fight of corruption difficult. For example, Section 19 of the Act declares that prosecuting a public officer charged with corruption is only effective with the written consent of the director of public prosecution, but written consent is often difficult to acquire. The PCB is assigned to investigate acts of corruption and thereafter submit the evidence gathered to the DPP, which decides whether or not to prosecute suspects. This makes people call PCB a toothless agency for failing to fight corruption, especially that which involves big shots.

For an alternative perspective, read the critical peer review commentary on this notebook, part of the 2006 Global Integrity Report (www.globalintegrity.org).

Uganda:
Leaders Who Overstay

By Salim R. Biryetega

In January 1986, as Ugandans prepared to swear in a new president, many believed the country was about to enter era, one in which abuse and misuse of public office would come to an end.

"The problems of Africa, and Uganda in particular, are caused by leaders who overstay in power, which breeds impunity, corruption and promotes patronage," President Yoweri Museveni said in his inauguration address.

Since that famous speech twenty years ago, some progress has been made. Key institutions such as the Inspectorate of Government were created, the Directorate of Public Prosecution was given autonomy, and government accountability and transparency laws were created, strengthened and expanded.

And yet, corruption remains rampant in each and every sector of Uganda.

The president, who has never lost a motion in

parliament, gets what he wants at all costs. In 2005, Members of Parliament were openly bribed with US$2,800 each to change a clause in the 1995 constitution that limited a president to two terms. (Museveni had already been re-elected in 1996 and 2001.) The term limit was lifted by Parliament, allowing the president who once decried "leaders who overstay in power" to win a third post-constitution term in February 2006.

But political patronage is not exclusive to the presidency. Corruption touches every institution in Uganda, from the private sector to the courts to health care. According to the second national integrity survey by the Inspectorate of Government, the most tainted sector is the police force, followed by the Uganda Revenue Authority and the magistrates courts.

Henry Muguzi, spokesman for the Anti Corruption Coalition Uganda (ACCU), said corruption has increased in Uganda, with the situation made worse by the public's tolerance of it.

"The corrupt are still regarded in high esteem, even in churches and mosques because they are the ones who can make huge offerings," Muguzi said.

Estimates of the scale of Uganda's corruption problem vary, but none paint a pretty picture. Uganda's Public Procurement and Disposal of Public Assets Authority (PPDA) estimates that over 330 billion shillings (US$184 million) is lost every year to corruption in procurement, which accounts for 70 percent of the government's annual budget. An estimate by the Uganda Debt Network puts the amount lost to corruption at 200 billion shillings (US$108 million) annually. Paul Onapa, spokesman for Transparency International's Uganda chapter, believes more than half of government funds are lost to corruption. That figure that would total a staggering 1.76 trillion shillings (US$950 million).

Those losses dramatically affect Uganda's economy, said Jasper Tumuhibise, an advocate with ACCU. Currently 51 percent of the Uganda's national budget is funded by donors, but Tumuhibise believes the national government could sustain itself if all revenues collected were properly utilized and not lost to corruption.

But graft is only one side of Uganda's corruption story. Sources in the Immigration Department, who did not want to be named for fear of reprisal, report widespread bribery in their agency. Foreigners, especially fake investors and political dissidents, can easily obtain work permits, passports and visas for the right payoff. Several top officials in the department were arrested in August 2006 and Museveni ordered an investigation. However, such anti-corruption efforts often are openly ridiculed by powerful people in the government. The minister of local government, Kahinda Otafiire, recently accused the inspector general of government, Lady Justice Faith Mwondha, of being drunk while writing a report that implicated him in scandalous land deals.

Uganda's corruption problem directly affects its ability to deal with its most serious problems.

In 2004, the Geneva-based Global Fund awarded Uganda $367 million in grants over two years to fight AIDS,

UGANDA

The Global Integrity Index:
How effective are Uganda's
anti-corruption safeguards?

OVERALL RATING

Moderate (76)

CATEGORY RATINGS

1) Civil Society, Public Information & Media — Strong (81)

2) Elections — Moderate (74)

3) Government Accountability — Moderate (76)

4) Administration & Civil Service — Moderate (71)

5) Oversight & Regulation — Strong (81)

6) Anti-Corruption & Rule of Law — Moderate (72)

(Scores range from 0 to 100)

The Global Integrity Index, through the Integrity Indicators, assesses the existence and effectiveness of national anti-corruption mechanisms. It does not measure corruption itself (which is nearly impossible). Instead, the Index analyzes the opposite of corruption: the institutions and practices that promote more accountable government and prevent, deter or punish corruption.

The Index is based on nearly 300 Integrity Indicators, discrete scores assigned by local experts using a consistent methodology and scoring criteria for each country. These results are then blindly peer reviewed at the local and international level to ensure consistency and accuracy.

All of the more than 11,000 Integrity Indicator scores that comprise the 2006 Index are published—along with extensive commentary, references and critical peer review comments and perspectives—in the annual Global Integrity Report.

For full results and downloadable datasets, see the Global Integrity website (www.globalintegrity.org).

tuberculosis and malaria. The grants, which amount to nearly 20 percent of the country's annual government spending, were intended to strengthen health systems and pay for diagnostics, mosquito nets and other necessities.

But in August 2005, an audit by Pricewaterhouse-Coopers found management irregularities serious enough to prompt the Global Fund to suspend the grants pending a government investigation and housecleaning. The revelation caused a scandal in Uganda.

An investigation commissioned by Museveni discovered that the minister of health, Jim Muhwezi, and two junior ministers had mismanaged the grants, including siphoning off for personal and political use money meant to help dying Ugandans.

The inquiry revealed that the Ugandan agency handling the Global Fund money had doled out grants to fake organizations, inflated the cost of workshops for staff and forged accountability documents. Funds were misused for staff members to study abroad, and briefcase non-governmental organizations were formed to absorb the AIDS money, with no actual work being done.

In its report to the president at the end of the inquiry in June 2006, the commission recommended that the health ministers be held accountable for the influence peddling and favoritism that led to the project's mismanagement and that all those who wrongly received money refund it or face financial or legal consequences.

Museveni sacked all three health ministers, a move that has been welcomed by many Ugandans, but they want to see tough action on the embezzlers of the AIDS money. People found guilty of misappropriating Global Fund grants were ordered to refund the money into a special Central Bank account. As of mid-August 2006, the account held US$540,000.

Museveni's response to the Global Fund scandal followed up on a promise he made during a May 2006 inaugural address. He said he would fight rampant corruption in government, including in his own National Resistance Movement party, and also streamline the corruption-tainted Immigration Department. However, his hard line was quickly questioned when, in forming his cabinet, he tapped his younger brother, Salim Saleh, whose government service has been dogged by many corruption scandals.

Another threat to reform is a law, in place since 1989, that requires nongovernmental organizations to register with the government. NGOs are subject to annual review by a board that includes government security officials. The implication is that any NGO that crosses the government can be declared illegal and evicted from the country.

Ashaba Aheebwa, Museveni's director of ethics and integrity, attributes the rampant corruption in the public sector to poor compensation of public officials. "Many people believe that when one gets a job in government, it's a ticket to riches," he said.

Civil society in Uganda has not developed a culture of advocacy and lobbying Aheebwa said, adding that until those practices gain traction and politics are abandoned, the fight against corruption will be futile.

Aheebwa said the country's media also have culpability for the corruption problem. "The media has not played its role of educating, informing and entertaining the public, but instead it acts as an opposition political group," he said.

Tumuhibise, of the ACCU, also believes that Ugandan news organizations are yet to appreciate that they have a duty to investigate, report and highlight corruption. "The media needs a complete turnaround on matters of corruption" he said.

For an alternative perspective, read the critical peer review commentary on this notebook, part of the 2006 Global Integrity Report (www.globalintegrity.org).

UGANDA

United States:
The Quiet Death of Ethics
By Jim Morris

The United States government is often quick to
denounce corruption and promote American-style democracy
in other countries. Recent events in Washington, however,
have shown that the U.S. has its own work to do to clean up
its government. The list of public officials who have admitted
to or are accused of accepting bribes or otherwise abusing
their positions is long. Here are just a few of the unseemly
developments during the first half of 2006:

In January, former lobbyist Jack Abramoff—closely
linked to onetime House Majority Leader Tom DeLay, R-
Texas—pleaded guilty to fraud, tax evasion and conspiracy
to bribe public officials on behalf of Indian tribes and other
clients. He was sentenced to five years and 10 months in
prison in March. DeLay, under indictment himself for alleged
involvement in campaign money laundering, resigned from
Congress in June.

In March, former congressman Randy "Duke"

Cunningham, R-Calif., was sentenced to eight years and four
months in prison for accepting $2.4 million in bribes from
defense contractors in exchange for government business.

In April, Rep. Alan Mollohan, D-W. Va., abandoned
his seat on the House Committee on Standards of Official
Conduct—commonly known as the ethics committee—amid
allegations that he improperly directed government funds
to foundations in his state, to his own financial benefit.
Mollohan has denied wrongdoing.

In May, Vernon Jackson, chief executive officer of iGate
Inc., a Kentucky-based telecommunications firm, pleaded
guilty to paying $400,000 in bribes to Rep. William Jefferson,
D-La., in exchange for Jefferson's help with deals in Africa.
The FBI said it found $90,000 of the money in a freezer in
Jefferson's home. As of early September, the congressman
had yet to be formally charged with any crime. Jackson was
sentenced to seven years and three months in prison.

Also in May, Neil Volz, a former aide to Rep. Bob Ney,
R-Ohio, and an erstwhile Abramoff associate, testified in
federal court that he was given free meals, tickets to sporting
events and other gifts by lobbyists when he was working for
the congressman. In return, Volz said, "I gave preferential
treatment to my lobbying buddies." In September, Ney—
implicated in the Abramoff scandal—agreed to plead guilty
to corruption charges. He could receive a prison term of up to
10 years and a fine of up to $500,000.

The opprobrium was not limited to Congress. It extended
to the states as well: After a six-month federal trial, the former
Republican Governor of Illinois, George Ryan, was convicted
in April of taking money, gifts and free travel in exchange for

UNITED STATES

The Global Integrity Index:
How effective are the United States' anti-corruption safeguards?

OVERALL RATING
Strong (87)

CATEGORY RATINGS

1) Civil Society, Public Information & Media — Strong (86)

2) Elections — Strong (83)

3) Government Accountability — Strong (88)

4) Administration & Civil Service — Strong (87)

5) Oversight & Regulation — Strong (86)

6) Anti-Corruption & Rule of Law — Very Strong (92)

(Scores range from 0 to 100)

The Global Integrity Index, through the Integrity Indicators, assesses the existence and effectiveness of national anti-corruption mechanisms. It does not measure corruption itself (which is nearly impossible). Instead, the Index analyzes the opposite of corruption: the institutions and practices that promote more accountable government and prevent, deter or punish corruption.

The Index is based on nearly 300 Integrity Indicators, discrete scores assigned by local experts using a consistent methodology and scoring criteria for each country. These results are then blindly peer reviewed at the local and international level to ensure consistency and accuracy.

All of the more than 11,000 Integrity Indicator scores that comprise the 2006 Index are published—along with extensive commentary, references and critical peer review comments and perspectives—in the annual Global Integrity Report.

For full results and downloadable datasets, see the Global Integrity website (www.globalintegrity.org).

government contracts and sentenced in September to 6 ½ years in prison. And the executive branch of the federal government is not without its own problems. For example, in a report released in June, the Senate Indian Affairs Committee raised questions about contacts between Abramoff and former deputy Interior Secretary J. Steven Griles.

Back in January, it appeared that the cascade of malfeasance from Capitol Hill would prompt significant reform. House Speaker Dennis Hastert, R-Ill., suggested a ban on privately funded travel for lawmakers and their staffs, in a tacit acknowledgement that some "fact-finding missions" are really high-dollar vacations, sponsored by corporations and others with business before Congress. The idea never gained momentum, perhaps because both Republicans and Democrats make wide use of these trips.

Lobbying and ethics reform bills in the House and the Senate proposed, among other things, a ban on gifts and full, online disclosure of lobbyist fundraising activities. These, too, went nowhere.

"It has been a striking year," said Mary Boyle, a spokeswoman for the watchdog group Common Cause. The litany of indictments and convictions, Boyle said, has been a predictable outcome of the "pay-to-play culture" fostered by DeLay and his brethren, who concocted the "K Street Project"—a largely successful attempt to pack lobbying firms with Republicans. This created "a unique environment, even by Washington standards" that allowed lobbyists to become more intimately involved in the legislative process, she said.

The upshot has been one scandal after another. But there have been no substantive attempts to fix the underlying problems, notably the rising costs of what appear to be perpetual campaigns and the impotence of the House and Senate ethics committees.

Melanie Sloan, executive director of Citizens for Responsibility and Ethics in Washington, sees "no prospect for lobbying reform. They [members of Congress] really don't want it."

But Sloan, a former federal prosecutor, isn't sure that new restrictions are the answer, anyway. "Creating new rules is completely useless if you don't enforce the ones you have," she said, noting that the ethics committees "are completely moribund."

Sloan and others have suggested that an independent Office of Public Integrity, along the lines of an inspector general in the executive branch, be created to do the dirty work the ethics committees are unable or unwilling to do themselves: Pass judgment on the propriety of privately sponsored trips, lobbyists' behavior and other sensitive matters.

The odds of that happening, she quickly added, are "absolutely nil."

If there was a glimmer of light during the dark days of 2005-06, Sloan said, it was the fact that some miscreants were actually getting caught. Prosecutors stepped in, she said, when it became obvious that Congress wasn't going to police itself.

Tom Fitton, president of the conservative-leaning Judicial Watch, noticed the same phenomenon. Within the past year or so, Fitton said, the Department of Justice has shown a willingness to prosecute public corruption cases it once might have avoided.

This, he believes, is a very good thing. "The best

possible reform is throwing politicians in jail," Fitton said. "That will do the most to keep them honest."

However, Craig Holman, the campaign finance lobbyist for the advocacy group founded by former Green Party presidential candidate Ralph Nader, argued that legislative remedies are needed. He said he is hopeful that they will be embraced by the next Congress.

Holman noted that the 2006 reform measures failed by small margins in most cases. He's convinced that the removal of a dozen or so "anti-reform incumbents" from Congress would allow key elements of those measures—including the establishment of an Office of Public Integrity and strict limits on privately funded travel—to be pushed through.

A noteworthy piece of legislation, designed to clean up what some believe to be an increasingly venal system of electing presidents, already has been introduced by Sen. Russ Feingold, D-Wis. The bill would greatly increase public funding of presidential campaigns, with the aim of eliminating or reducing the advantage held by candidates who raise vast amounts of private money (and are, therefore, beholden to their big contributors). Public Citizen found that the two candidates in 2004, George W. Bush and John Kerry, raised $262 million and $248 million, respectively, from private sources.

In early September, a separate bill was being drafted to boost public funding of congressional campaigns. Like candidates for the White House, members of Congress are awash in private money. Public Citizen recently reported that lobbyists and their political action committees had contributed at least $103 million to lawmakers since 1998.

UNITED STATES

"Such enormous sums buy commensurate access, shutting most Americans out of the process and skewing legislation and budget allocation," the group's president, Joan Claybrook, said in a press statement.

The president of Common Cause, Chellie Pingree, told the House Committee on Government Reform in February that the metastasizing scandals had "greatly frayed" Americans' faith in their government. "The spectacle of executive branch officials and members of Congress betraying their duty to serve the public interest increases public cynicism and threatens to erode further citizen participation in our democracy," Pingree testified.

At the time she gave her statement, support for meaningful change was at its zenith. Jack Abramoff had just entered his guilty plea and promised to cooperate with investigators, providing names of members of Congress and aides he had sought to influence. Craig Holman's phone was "ringing off the hook," he said, as lawmakers solicited feedback on reform legislation.

"Suddenly, this reform movement just took off on its own," Holman said. "I was exceedingly optimistic at the beginning of this year."

As the months went by, however, "all these calls for huge, sweeping reforms . . . just faded away," Holman said wistfully. It was almost as if the Abramoff affair had never happened.

For an alternative perspective, read the critical peer review commentary on this notebook, part of the 2006 Global Integrity Report (www.globalintegrity.org).

Vietnam:
Pervasive and Consuming

*By Global Integrity**

"Never marry a policeman," my father always warns me. Many other young ladies in Vietnam get the same advice from their parents. Ordinary Vietnamese people are learning to dislike the police. The reason is simple. Experience from day-to-day life teaches us that the more you encounter the police, the more you have to bribe.

"You violated the traffic law. What do you want me to do?" the policeman asked me after I was caught stopping in the wrong lane on a busy street in Hanoi.

"What should I do?" I replied.

"You must know. I need to buy a cup of tea or maybe a cigarette."

"How much?"

"I will do you a favor. Give me only 48,000 dong (US$3). Put your money in this traffic ticket book, so no one can see it," he said and smiled.

* *The author is a Vietnamese journalist who reqested his/her name be witheheld, citing the potential threat of government recrimination.*

If I didn't accept the "favor" from that policeman, my motorbike might be confiscated for 15 days. After two weeks without means of transport, I would pay a fine of 208,000 dong (US$13) and an extra 240,000 dong (US$15) stocking fee, then 16,000 dong (US$1) per day and finally go through a very complicated procedure to get back my motorbike, which would be in remarkably bad shape. The police have no room to store so many confiscated motorbikes, so they are normally left outside, exposed to the sun, rain and the generally humid weather of a tropical country. What choice do I have?

Traffic police can make a lot of money because traffic in Vietnam is terrible; people frequently violate the law. One reason is because you don't need to learn traffic law to get a driver's license. Two months ago, my nephew, Hung, turned 18 and "took" a test to get his driver's license. He passed the driver's test without knowing anything about driving law because he paid a 320,000 dong (US$20) bribe. Almost everyone pays bribes for a driver's license. Without the bribe, it may take six months or more to obtain a license. It took Hung only two weeks.

At the end of last year, the Central Internal Board of the Communist Party carried out a Sweden-sponsored research study on corruption. The study revealed that paying bribes is now a habit of the Vietnamese; 71.2 percent of people in Hanoi and 67.4 percent of people in Ho Chi Minh City, the two biggest cities in Vietnam, are willing to bribe to get things done. Meanwhile, one third of the government workforce interviewed admits receiving bribes.

Some people may insist on never paying bribes. But while they can wait for driver's licenses, can they wait for medical or educational services?

We have a tradition of offering flowers to teachers during Teachers' Day. However, instead of flowers, we now have to give money. The amount of money, from 80,000 dong (US$5) to 320,000 dong (US$20), depends on whether the student has rich or poor parents. With this small envelope of money, parents know their child will receive much better care. "Because most teachers are women, now I have to give money on International Women's Day, Vietnamese Women's Day and even New Year's Day," complained Hoa, whose 4-year-old son is attending a public kindergarten.

The prospects are even gloomier for Hoa while her child grows up. One of my friends had to pay 8 million dong (US$500) to get her child into a good public primary school. And if that child gets good marks at a good school and is qualified to attend university or college, he might have to pay bribes, or else enter an unequal race there. My cousin is studying at National Economics University, which is the dream university of many high school students. One day, he asked his parents for money, saying, "I need money to pass this exam. I didn't do well on my last test. I'll pass if I give the teacher 208,000 dong (US$13)."

His father was so surprised: "How do you know that your teacher will take your money?"

"Many of my friends gave the teacher money and they got good marks."

That's why I was not surprised when I recently read in

VIETNAM

The Global Integrity Index:
How effective are Vietnam's
anti-corruption safeguards?

OVERALL RATING

Very Weak (47)

CATEGORY RATINGS

1) Civil Society, Public Information & Media — Very Weak (28)

2) Elections — Very Weak (39)

3) Government Accountability — Very Weak (33)

4) Administration & Civil Service — Very Weak (54)

5) Oversight & Regulation — Very Weak (57)

6) Anti-Corruption & Rule of Law — Weak (70)

(Scores range from 0 to 100)

The Global Integrity Index, through the Integrity Indicators, assesses the existence and effectiveness of national anti-corruption mechanisms. It does not measure corruption itself (which is nearly impossible). Instead, the Index analyzes the opposite of corruption: the institutions and practices that promote more accountable government and prevent, deter or punish corruption.

The Index is based on nearly 300 Integrity Indicators, discrete scores assigned by local experts using a consistent methodology and scoring criteria for each country. These results are then blindly peer reviewed at the local and international level to ensure consistency and accuracy.

All of the more than 11,000 Integrity Indicator scores that comprise the 2006 Index are published—along with extensive commentary, references and critical peer review comments and perspectives—in the annual Global Integrity Report.

For full results and downloadable datasets, see the Global Integrity website (www.globalintegrity.org).

the newspapers that some government officials neither went to class, nor wrote a theses, yet still received doctorates.

Going to see a doctor is a nightmare for the poor. All the big hospitals in Vietnam are public. Doctors and nurses behave as if they were government officials. One day, I went to the hospital to visit my uncle who was a patient there. I felt so ashamed when I heard a nurse shouting at a very sick, old lady from the countryside: "Get out of here!" she yelled, "You can't sit here, you filthy woman." The nurse's behavior would be very different if that had been a rich woman who was willing to pay bribes.

The most lucrative business around hospitals is making change. People need small change to bribe nurses and doctors. If someone wants a less painful injection that is more carefully given, or wants to change to cleaner hospital clothes, he or she must pay 800 dong (US 50 cents). If a patient wants to be examined earlier without waiting in a very long queue of patients, the patient needs to either be a relative or acquaintance of the nurses and doctors, or pay 16,000 dong (US$1) to 32,000 dong (US$2). If a patient pays 48,000 dong (US$3), the doctor will examine the patient more carefully. And the amount of bribe might reach 800,000 dong (US $50) to 3.2 million dong (US$200) or more if a patient has a serious disease or has to go through surgery.

Ordinary people have to bribe because they want to have better service and medical care. Virtually all government staff accept bribes because they want to earn more money. The average monthly salary for an experienced doctor at a public hospital is around 1,600,000 dong (US$100). A nurse earns

800,000 dong (US$50) per month.

Doctors and nurses must also pay bribes. My friend who graduated from Hanoi Medical University secretly paid 160 million dong (US$10,000) to get a job at a big hospital in Hanoi.

We often say, "In Vietnam, everybody has a salary but no one lives on it." That's why corruption is so common among officials, from low- to high-ranking ones.

At the beginning of 2006, Vietnamese people were shocked when a newspaper reported that Bui Tien Dung, executive director of Project Management Unit 18 (PMU) of the Ministry of Transportation (MOT) spent 36 billion dong (US$2.3 million) gambling on soccer. The average annual salary in Vietnam is no more than 8 million dong (US$500) per year.

An average salary of an official like the director of PMU 18 is just 3.2 million dong (US$200) to 4.8 million dong (US$300) per month, or 57 million dong (US$3,600) per year. So where did that huge amount of gambling money come from?

PMU 18 is one of 23 PMUs, which manage all transportation projects. PMU 18 is in charge of projects related to Official Development Aid (ODA), which foreign donors lent Vietnam with preferential interest rates. Last year, Vietnam received record-high ODA funding of 48 trillion dong (US$3 billion). The majority of that money was invested in infrastructure projects including building roads and bridges. A newspaper found out that many projects managed by PMU 18 were badly done because the officials at PMU 18 skimmed off money and took kickbacks from lucrative state contracts.

This reveals the difficulties facing most businesses in Vietnam. They win few government contracts unless they offer kickbacks to government officials. According to the Vietnam Chamber of Commerce and Industry, 77 percent of businesses in Hanoi (highest percentage) and 12 percent of businesses in Binh Duong provinces (lowest percentage) pay "commissions" to government officials. As a matter of course, the higher the kickbacks, the worse the quality of the completed projects. The Vietnam Youth newspaper (*Thanh Nien*) quoted a Vietnamese economist who stated, "Corruption is consuming 3 percent to 4 percent of Vietnam's Gross Domestic Product. Without corruption, the growth rate of Vietnam would have been 9 percent to 10 percent."

Recently, Politburo member Phan Dien said that corruption is a danger even for the party and the survival of political system. Dung, several other lower transport officials and the Vice Minister of Transport were detained. The Minister of Transport resigned. Some officials in Ministry of Police (MOP) were arrested on suspicion of taking bribes to protect the notorious PMU director. Even a major general in MOP, head of Vietnam's police investigation unit, lost his job.

This is the biggest corruption scandal ever revealed in Vietnam. Newspapers have played a big role in bringing the scandal to light. This reflects a big shift because all the news media in Vietnam are owned by the government. Many newspapers, both print and online versions, included public opinion expressing anger over this terrible corruption. Tens

VIETNAM

of millions of Vietnamese people will have to work to pay for the loan that officials have squandered. People are worried that corruption is entrenched across the whole system.

How could Dung steal that much money if he didn't have the support of, or conspire with other officials?

An anti-corruption law took effect last June: an anti-corruption agency will be established and the Prime Minister will be the head of this agency. Public opinion has already started asking who will make sure the agency itself isn't corrupt. What if the anti-corruption agency's staff is corrupt? Who will be held responsible?

Whomever I'll marry, a policeman, a doctor or an employee of a foreign company who has never had a chance to be corrupted, my parents now have a new worry. My child, their grandchild, on his or her first day in life, will bear a huge burden of debt left by the previous irresponsible generation.

For an alternative perspective, read the critical peer review commentary on this notebook, part of the 2006 Global Integrity Report (www.globalintegrity.org).

West Bank:
Governing at Gunpoint

By Issa Sharabati

"One can accept that the government sometimes blackmails or harasses its citizens. But it is almost surreal to discover that citizens have started blackmailing their formal institutions," said Abdel Naser, 48, a taxi driver in the city of Ramallah. He spoke while watching 40 gunmen congregate. The gunmen identified themselves as members of the Al-Aqsa Martyr Brigades—the military wing of the Fatah party.

On April 14, 2006, the Alaqsa Martyrs gathered on a busy street in Ramallah and stormed into the Ministry of Transportation. The gunmen were headed by Muin Aljubii, who demanded to speak to new transportation minister Ziad Althatha, a member of the Hamas party. Althatha had been appointed only a week earlier, following Hamas' sweep of the Palestinian elections.

"We came to protest the failure of the ministry to pay the salaries of families of the...wounded and martyrs of the *intifada* [uprising]," Aljubii announced to the bewildered bureaucrats. Althatha wasn't even there; he was based in Gaza. Officials in the building didn't understand why the gunmen choose transportation of all possible ministries as the target of their demands.

Aljubii went on to explain that the previous minister, a Fatah leader, made them a promise before the elections. The Ministry of Transportation would allocate special plates for taxis to Fatah activists as compensation for their role in the Palestinian *intifada*. Simultaneous attacks were occurring at branches of the ministry in the West Bank cities of Nablus and Tul Karm.

A taxi plate is a treasure in Palestine. Sixty percent of Palestinians earn fewer than two dollars per day, but a taxi plate, which licenses its owner to work as a driver, can bring in an annual salary of 30,500 new sheqalim (US$7,000). Though Aljubii spoke for the martyrs and the wounded, in fact he represents the biggest business in Palestine these days: armed political gangs.

The gunmen are mostly Fatah activists already on the Palestinian Authority (PA) payroll, sometimes with ordinary criminals thrown in. They blackmail the PA on a daily basis. The pretexts vary, but always contain patriotism and national slogans.

"This is a transportation ministry. We are not a charity association, and we don't allocate anything for the families of the poor," said Althatha, who was shocked by the incident. "These requests are nothing but a blackmail attempts that we will not give in to." A day after the incident, another gang stormed the Ministry of Health in Gaza to demand medical treatment for a cancer patient, killing an official.

Other groups kidnap foreign journalists or aid workers all over the West Bank and Gaza. Their ransom demand? Jobs with the PA, which is under pressure from foreign governments to put a stop to the chaos and anarchy.

Althatha may seek good governance, but shortly after his appointment he discovered that he didn't have any practical authority due to the economic blockade on the PA following the Hamas electoral victory.

As a Hamas official, Althatha has an interest in slandering the old Fatah regime. Nevertheless, documents and statements from the officials in his office show that the ministry he inherited has no less than 40 "general directors" on salary. Some of them are never seen in the office, yet earn 8,722 new sheqalim (US$2,000) a month.

Similarly, new religious affairs minister and Hamas member Sheikh Naef Rajub discovered that a week before he started the job, the previous minister appointed 19 new "general directors," some without any professional skills or experience.

One of these "general directors" had earlier been accused of corruption, arrested by security services and suspended from duty. After the Hamas victory, however, he was reappointed to the same ministry and position. Hamas, now struggling to survive the political clash with Fatah, doesn't dare fire anyone aligned with Fatah, corrupt or otherwise. Furious, Rajub said to me just before he was arrested: "I could only transfer [the director] to a marginal position—seventy meters from his original office."

The issue of taxi plates may sound likes an aside to larger battles, but it is a striking example of the corruption in all the PA ministries. Documents show that former transportation minister Saad a-did Hurma issued an order in March 2005 to stop distributing plates because of the huge number of taxis already operating in the West Bank.

Two months later, Hurma established a professional committee comprised of five ministry officials and two security forces officers (which would benefit from the distribution of new plates) to reevaluate the situation. The committee determined that the number of taxis already operating was 22 percent higher than needed, concluding that no taxi plates should be distributed until 2011.

In June 2005, the committee offered this warning: "It is crucial that the ministry of transportation will not consider any humanitarian needs as to the requests for taxi plates because the ministry is not a ministry for social affairs or assistance for the poor. Further allocations will result in economic and personal catastrophe for the existing drivers and to the economy in general."

The Palestinian Central Bureau of Statistics offered not to distribute more than 122 plates a year under any circumstances until 2007. Other aides to the minister warned him against issuing more plates.

Yet as late as October 2005, Hurma began distributing plates in large numbers, authorizing 433 new ones by the end of 2005. On March 3rd, 2006, a few days before the declaration of the new Hamas government and arrival of the new minister, Althatha handed out 542 new plates in one day!

The gunmen who came to the Ministry of Transportation this April did so only because they had done it for years. For the last 11 years, Fatah was the PA and the PA was Fatah. Fatah activists were appointed to public sector positions according to their organizational status.

They also were guests in all ministries and governmental departments, with economic privilege to match their status. Taxi plates are only one example: They could get nearly anything they wanted. The arrival of the new Hamas government, specifically the new minister of transportation, was a shock. Hamas was suddenly a threat after long years of Fatah domination.

The Al-Aqsa martyrs were terrified of loosing those privileges, so this time they showed up with their guns.

"We have more taxis than people here," said Althatha. "The professionals in the ministry are saying that no new plates should be distributed until the year 2010, [yet] I found out that the ministry gave 500 plates to different groups. Sometimes they would be given to associates of officials, sometimes to members of the security forces and sometimes to gangs like the one who stormed the office in Ramallah."

"Right now, everything is frozen," said Althatha. "I hope that it will improve in the future."

For an alternative perspective, read the critical peer review commentary on this notebook, part of the 2006 Global Integrity Report (www.globalintegrity.org).

WEST BANK

Republic of Yemen:
How to Buy Qat
By Walid Al-Saqaf

If you have ever visited the Republic of Yemen before, you may well have heard about "*hag-al-gat.*" This term literally means "money to buy *qat.*" This phrase is a well-established protocol for demanding a bribe.

Qat is a narcotic plant. Its leaves are chewed by the majority of Yemeni adults near the end of every day across Yemen, where 40 percent of the population lives below the poverty line.

If a traffic policeman stops you near a traffic light and asks for *hag-al-gat,* he is politely asking you for a bribe. In exchange, he will not issue you a ticket. Don't try to argue, just give him 500 rial (US$3) and avoid a long and painful argument with one or, perhaps eventually, several traffic policemen.

Unlike other countries around the world, there are no standards that could be used to define how much a *hag-al-gat* would be for a specific duty. It largely depends on the amount of work the person requesting the bribe is willing to do, along with his mood and possibly your tribal or political affiliation. It may cost 100 rial (US$0.50) to get a document notarized in a small police station and rise to millions of rial handed in sacks to a judge in order to reverse a verdict that is about to be issued in his court.

Of course, to secure the verdict even further, perhaps a few bundles of fresh and expensive Hamdani *qat* may help as well. *Qat* constitutes the second largest household expense for an average Yemeni family, often taking up a third of the family's budget. The Yemeni economy posts a 250 billion rial (US$1.2 billion) annual loss due to the consumption of this narcotic. To counteract this, the government has initiated a five-year plan to eradicate *qat*.

On the other hand, *hag-al-gat* has helped plenty of people, including Ali Al-Saman, who was saved from unemployment because of *hag-al-gat*. In a country that suffers from a staggering 35 percent unemployment rate, Ali knew, with his 62 percent high school score, there was no way he could get a decent job. After struggling for months to find work, Ali was told he could buy a life-long governmental post for as little as 150,000 rial (US$759). He took his chances and paid *hag-al-gat*. Today, he enjoys a decent government position and a new career.

During his school years, Ahmed would pay fees to his school to help pay to paint the classroom or renovate a laboratory, and so on. He never saw the implementation of those pledges and often wondered why. As he grew up, he realized that the school management and teachers were pocketing the money. He never dared to complain, because he

The Global Integrity Index:
How effective are the Republic of Yemen's anti-corruption safeguards?

OVERALL RATING
Very Weak (49)

CATEGORY RATINGS

1) Civil Society, Public Information & Media — Very Weak (41)

2) Elections — Very Weak (55)

3) Government Accountability — Very Weak (38)

4) Administration & Civil Service — Very Weak (53)

5) Oversight & Regulation — Very Weak (46)

6) Anti-Corruption & Rule of Law — Very Weak (60)

(Scores range from 0 to 100)

The Global Integrity Index, through the Integrity Indicators, assesses the existence and effectiveness of national anti-corruption mechanisms. It does not measure corruption itself (which is nearly impossible). Instead, the Index analyzes the opposite of corruption: the institutions and practices that promote more accountable government and prevent, deter, or punish corruption.

The Index is based on nearly 300 Integrity Indicators, discrete scores assigned by local experts using a consistent methodology and scoring criteria for each country. These results are then blindly peer reviewed at the local and international level to ensure consistency and accuracy.

All of the more than 11,000 Integrity Indicator scores that comprise the 2006 Index are published—along with extensive commentary, references and critical peer review comments and perspectives—in the annual Global Integrity Report.

For full results and downloadable datasets, see the Global Integrity website (www.globalintegrity.org).

knew he would be asking for trouble. In fact, he asked me not to publish his last name, fearing consequences from school management. (Most of the people interviewed for this story were unwilling to have their names published for similar reasons.)

The Yemeni press has published many stories about corruption in education, sometimes with disastrous consequences for the journalists involved. A Yemeni newspaper, Al-Wasat, was sued and its editor-in-chief kidnapped by armed forces after publishing the names of the sons of government officials. The paper alleged that these students were improperly granted academic scholarships to study abroad.

Just as education is heavily infested with corruption, so is the health sector. According to a medical doctor, surgeries funded by international donors to support the poor are actually sold by public officials. Meanwhile, a professional at a public hospital told me that the cashier deducts at least 0.1 percent of the monthly salaries of most employees. "This may seem a small amount," she said, "but when added up for all the 1,000-plus employees in the hospital, it amounts to more than two times his own salary."

I spoke with a cashier, Abubakr, who works with a large army unit in the capital, Sanaa. He had nothing but good news to report.

"God has blessed me with a luxurious life, many real estate properties and brand new cars," he said with pride, adding that his boss is quite happy with his performance. He is responsible for distributing salaries to a list of missing

YEMEN

people and made-up names. They don't really get paid, of course. Every month, he transfers about 18 million rial (US$91,100) to his manager.

It is believed that corruption in the army, which receives close to 200 billion rial (US$1 billion) in aid annually, is on a mammoth scale, but the regime's unwillingness to reveal detailed expense reports makes tracking the embezzled money a serious challenge.

Abdullah works for the army and enjoys lots of financial resources from the military budget. When a batch of cars arrives at the military camp under the names of "imaginary" soldiers, most of those cars go directly to the top military officers. Some get sold on the black market.

"I sometimes get a decent commission selling a car," Abdullah said, adding that he is also allowed free gasoline and diesel daily.

Small-scale corruption takes place daily in various governmental institutions, including the Tax and Customs Authorities. According to Nasser, who works as a collector for the Tax Authority, his district sends about 3 million rial (US$15,179) to the authority monthly. The actual amount collected averages 13 million rial (US$65,776); meaning more than three quarters of the tax collected goes directly to the authority's crooks.

Meanwhile, it's another good day for Hamed, who works at the Customs Authority. "I've just received another 3,000 rial (US$15) for exempting a fellow from customs duty," he said, adding that this is nothing compared to the "millions" that the top officers at the authority get.

If you were importing goods into the country and wanted to avoid taxes or paperwork, you could pay an extra 25 percent to get your goods through without official documentation. As a result of these transactions, defective medicine has been smuggled into the country, right through official border points.

Many government employees envy those working at the Bids and Tenders Committee headed by the Minister of Finance. Bids and Tenders is a fertile ground for corruption and produces massive commissions, which can make crooked officials millionaires. This is precisely what happened to a committee member who was quite poor when he entered the committee years ago. Today he owns a villa worth 45 million rial (US$228,686) in a modern district of the capital.

Meanwhile, the business sector has learned to cope with these tenders and bids, and through bribes, gifts and other means, many are able to win deals regardless of their qualifications.

But Finance isn't the only ministry that presents opportunities for graft. One accounting department employee at the Ministry of Information reports that the more than 2 billion rial (US$10 million) is unaccounted for in his ministry. He expressed little hope of retrieving it or punishing those involved.

Ultimately, these examples are dwarfed when compared to the massive corruption taking place in the upper levels of the government, particularly when suspicious oil and international contracts are involved. It was recently revealed that 204 billion rial (US$1 billion) has been

YEMEN

illegally distributed, embezzled, uncollected or is otherwise
unaccounted for in the Parliament.

Despite his 28 years in power, President Ali Abdullah
Saleh confessed in many speeches that the time has come for
him to fight corruption. Until June 2006, Saleh resisted calls
to run for office again in the September 2006 presidential
elections, arguing that he did not want to be an "umbrella
for the corrupt."

But after deciding to enter the race, he ran on a platform
of uprooting corruption, a phenomenon that pervades every
government agency in this poverty-stricken country. Nearly
everyone shares this view. Opinion surveys by Transparency
International rank Yemen behind all countries in the Arabian
Peninsula, except Iraq and occupied Palestine.

The irony is that there are many cases of documented
corruption that could indict officials and their affiliates.
Each institution is arranged like dominos—just one nudge
could send the chain tumbling. However, legal action has
never taken place, not even once, which reinforces the
opinion that the government does not want any of these
officials to be prosecuted.

Those in power will never allow the dominos to fall for
fear that each, in turn, would knock the next, and the next,
until every last piece is taken down.

*For an alternative perspective, read the critical peer review com-
mentary on this notebook, part of the 2006 Global Integrity
Report (www.globalintegrity.org).*

Zimbabwe:
Zero Tolerance

By Njabulo Ncube

The pay slip of a civil servant in Zimbabwe bears the following inscription: "Live within your means; shun corruption."

Here in Zimbabwe, corruption in both the public and private sectors is endemic. In fact, things are so bad here that in 2005 President Robert Mugabe established an entirely new ministry, the Ministry of Anti-Corruption, as well as an Anti-Corruption Commission chaired by a former comptroller and auditor general.

Nevertheless, for Zimbabweans, graft is a part of life and death alike. Zimbabweans of all classes—from the ruling Zimbabwe African National Union Patriotic Front (ZANU PF) elite to the impoverished vast majority of the population—have no qualms whatsoever about bribing public servants to get documents such as birth certificates, national identity cards, passports—even death certificates.

The amount of the bribe varies according to the

importance of the document. A brown envelope with $10 million Zimbabwe dollars (US$41) secures most public documents available through the national registrar's office. However, passports, which are in great demand as impoverished Zimbabweans seek opportunities overseas and in neighboring South Africa and Botswana, command a steeper bribe in order to be processed in under a week.

Both petty and grand-scale corruption have been steadily increasing over the last five years, according to Transparency International of Zimbabwe (TIZ) and the African Parliamentarians Network Against Corruption (APNAC), two advocacy groups campaigning against graft.

Speaking in hushed tones, public officials say they need the bribes to supplement meager salaries in a country where the average person survives on less than a dollar per day.

Tobaiwa Mudede, the Registrar General, heads the national office that issues birth certificates, national identity cards, travel documents and other public documents. In January 2005, he fired eight senior passport officers for demanding bribes. "We have zero tolerance for corruption," Mudede told this reporter. The corruption is not only in public offices, but also in other sectors of the tottering economy, which is in its seventh consecutive year of recession. In 2005, several high-ranking banking, business and legal executives who were facing corruption charges fled the country and its anti-corruption dragnet, which has to date successfully prosecuted only petty offenders.

James Makamba, a former ruling party central committee member and ZANU PF legislator, jumped bail in August 2005 over allegations of externalizing foreign currency. High Court Judge Benjamin Paradza also skipped the country after being convicted on two counts of corruption for allegedly attempting to influence two other judges to release a passport of a business colleague facing murder charges.

Both the businessman and the judge, who are reportedly hiding out in the United Kingdom and New Zealand respectively, alleged political prosecution by President Mugabe's government—charges authorities in Harare, the capital city, vehemently deny.

When President Mugabe's favorite nephew, Leo Mugabe, was arrested in October 2005 for allegedly smuggling contraband valued at $150 billion Zimbabwe dollars (US$621,858) to Mozambique, impoverished Zimbabweans held hope that the government was finally cracking down on graft at the top. This was less than six months after the president spoke out against corruption and set up the Ministry of Anti-Corruption.

But three weeks later, Leo Mugabe was acquitted due to lack of incriminating evidence, despite the truckload of flour and fertilizer—contraband items under Zimbabwe law—that was impounded and traced to Mugabe's company. The items were later sold at public auction by Zimbabwe revenue authorities.

"People come up with all sort of allegations because I am related to the president," Mugabe told this reporter in an interview during which he denied involvement in the smuggling of goods to neighboring Mozambique.

The Global Integrity Index:
How effective are Zimbabwe's anti-corruption safeguards?

OVERALL RATING
Weak (64)

CATEGORY RATINGS

1) Civil Society, Public Information & Media — Weak (60)

2) Elections — Very Weak (50)

3) Government Accountability — Very Weak (52)

4) Administration & Civil Service — Weak (61)

5) Oversight & Regulation — Strong (86)

6) Anti-Corruption & Rule of Law — Moderate (78)

(Scores range from 0 to 100)

The Global Integrity Index, through the Integrity Indicators, assesses the existence and effectiveness of national anti-corruption mechanisms. It does not measure corruption itself (which is nearly impossible). Instead, the Index analyzes the opposite of corruption: the institutions and practices that promote more accountable government and prevent, deter or punish corruption.

The Index is based on nearly 300 Integrity Indicators, discrete scores assigned by local experts using a consistent methodology and scoring criteria for each country. These results are then blindly peer reviewed at the local and international level to ensure consistency and accuracy.

All of the more than 11,000 Integrity Indicator scores that comprise the 2006 Index are published—along with extensive commentary, references and critical peer review comments and perspectives—in the annual Global Integrity Report.

For full results and downloadable datasets, see the Global Integrity website (www.globalintegrity.org).

"These are my political enemies who are just jealous of my business and political success," he said. "I am not corrupt. My business dealing is above board. I have been acquitted by the courts of the land on the smuggling, and that's that."

Leo Mugabe says he does not understand why his name always pops up when graft or corruption scandals are written about in the local media. "I am not a litigious person. If I were, most newspapers would be in hot [water]," added Mugabe, who also was named in the controversy surrounding the construction of the new Harare International Airport in the early 1990s.

Anti-graft campaigners in Zimbabwe say that despite speaking out publicly against graft and setting up the Ministry of Anti-Corruption, President Mugabe's anti-corruption efforts seem fruitless, since the ministry has failed to take action or successfully prosecute any culprits.

In interviews with this reporter, anti-graft campaigners accused the president of not "walking the walk."

Since independence from colonial Britain, the campaigners pointed out, President Mugabe has set up several commissions to investigate corruption, but their findings have never been publicized because they involved either senior government officials or the rich.

The findings of the Willowvale car scandal (which became known as "Willowgate"), for example, in which government ministers acquired cars at concessionary rates and later sold them at exorbitant prices to unsuspecting members of the public, were somewhat swept under the carpet (though several ministers were ultimately forced to resign). Findings that the War Victims Compensation Fund was looted by government ministers and party officials, as well as accusations that President Mugabe's inner circle awarded themselves more than one farm each under the president's land reform program have also gone relatively unnoticed (though some veterans were ultimately compensated).

Sunsleey Chamunorwa, editor-in-chief of the country's leading financial and political weekly, has this advice for the Zimbabwean leader: "Actions speak louder than words, Mr. President," Chamunorwa wrote in one of his weekly columns. "To a visitor from Mars, President Mugabe easily passes for someone who takes umbrage at corruption if only public statements and their elaboration tones are anything to go by," he wrote. "To Zimbabweans, the sincerity, commitment and political will of President Mugabe's government to rid the country of corruption remains highly debatable."

Zimbabwe continues to score high on the corruption charts despite spirited attempts by Harare to root out the scourge pervasive in both the private and public sectors, added Chamunorwa, whose paper regularly exposes corruption.

Mary Jane, a researcher with Transparency International of Zimbabwe, says although the country has ratified various international protocols and entered into regional partnerships to fight corruption, it continues to move up the corruption barometer due to massive illegal deals, which have become the normal way of doing business.

"Much of the government's fight has proved to be only rhetoric as allegations of grand corruption cases involving high-level officials go uninvestigated and consequently unpunished," said Jane. "If investigations of corruption do not lead to prosecutions, then public confidence on the legitimacy of the government's political will to fight corruption wanes."

Kindness Paradza, the secretary general of APNAC and former ruling party legislator, added his thoughts on the state of corruption and accountability in Zimbabwe:

"The absence of the rule of law and poor governance are fueling graft with senior [ruling party officials] and ZANU PF officials [are] becoming immune to prosecution."

For an alternative perspective, read the critical peer review commentary on this notebook, part of the 2006 Global Integrity Report (www.globalintegrity.org).

ZIMBABWE

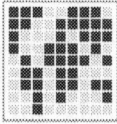

GLOBAL INTEGRITY
Independent Information on Governance & Corruption

www.globalintegrity.org

Global Integrity is an independent, non-profit organization tracking governance and corruption trends around the world. Global Integrity uses local teams of researchers and journalists to monitor openness and accountability.

With the expansion of democracy worldwide, the expectation that a government is accountable to its people, and there to serve the public interest, is the growing norm in every region of the world. Yet in many countries the ideal of accountable government falls short when corruption, abuses of power, electoral fraud and official secrecy undermine the promise of popular rule.

Global Integrity exposes this "democratic deficit" by assessing the existence and effectiveness of key governance institutions that are meant to protect and promote the public interest—we explore and report on the implementation gap between what is promised in law (*de jure*) and what is delivered in practice (*de facto*).

Our unique assessment methodology, applied on the ground by in-country expert social scientists and journalists, exposes the weaknesses in the institutional framework underpinning a government's commitment and capacity to truly deliver. Our credible, comprehensive, and timely data and reporting on corruption and accountability systems provide a clear way forward for reform-minded stakeholders seeking more responsive government.

Investment and development funding decisions are increasingly related to a country's performance on various scales of "good governance." The information that should inform those decisions is rarely available, however, let alone up-to-date. For those incentives to function properly, the international community needs a trustworthy source of independent information produced without partisan, ideological, or financial agendas. That data must based on a robust and transparent methodology, accepted by all stakeholders as a reliable tool for quantitatively and qualitatively gauging government accountability and openness. It must be comprehensive and timely, covering as many countries as possible and harvested regularly to ensure that reforms and inputs can be measured over time.

Global Integrity meets this demand. Global Integrity arms decision makers—whether government policymakers, emerging market investors, or grassroots advocates—with cutting-edge tools that identify unexpected trends and ground future decisions in trustworthy data and reporting. We help promote evidence-based decision making and provide actionable, "home-grown" information that simultaneously remains comparable across countries, regions, and internationally.

SPARKS
CUSTOM PUBLISHING

www.sparkscustom.com

Sparks Custom Publishing provided editorial support for more than 750,000 words of original content published in the 2006 Global Integrity Report, including this book.

Sparks offers turn-key communications support for non-profits and businesses, bringing in talented communications professionals to work on temporary or long-term engagements. By taking on a project management role, Sparks removes the hassle of hiring freelancers with less overhead than a traditional agency. Sparks offers its clients affordable access to high-quality communications services including writing, editing, design, brand consulting and production support.

A for-profit company, Sparks is committed to integrating social and environmental concerns into its bottom line. For details, see the Sparks website (www.sparkscustom.com).

www.ingramcontent.com/pod-product-compliance
Lightning Source LLC
Chambersburg PA
CBHW020605270326
41927CB00005B/179